KOMMANDO

KOMMANDO

Hitler's Special Forces in the Second World War

by

Charles Whiting

*'Even if we could not conquer, we should drag
half the world into destruction with us and leave
no one to triumph over Gemany . . . we may be
destroyed, but if we are, we shall drag the world
with us – A WORLD IN FLAMES'*

Josef Goebbels

Pen & Sword
MILITARY

First published in Great Britain in hardback in 1995 by
LEO COOPER
Reprinted in this format in 2010 by
Pen & Sword Military
an imprint of
Pen & Sword Books Ltd
47 Church Street
Barnsley
South Yorkshire   S70 2AS

ISBN 978 1 84884 275 5

The right of Charles Whiting to be identified as
author of this work has been asserted by him in accordance
with the Copyright, Designs and Patents Act 1988

A CIP catalogue record for this book is
available from the British Library

Printed and bound in England
by CPI Antony Rowe, Chippenham, Wiltshire

Pen & Sword Books Ltd incorporates the imprints of
Pen & Sword Aviation, Pen & Sword Maritime, Pen & Sword Military,
Wharncliffe Local History, Pen & Sword Select,
Pen & Sword Military Classics and Leo Cooper,
Remember When, Seaforth Publishing and Frontline Publishing

For a complete list of Pen & Sword titles please contact
PEN & SWORD BOOKS LIMITED
47 Church Street, Barnsley, South Yorkshire, S70 2AS, England
E-mail: enquiries@pen-and-sword.co.uk
Website: www.pen-and-sword.co.uk

CONTENTS

ACKNOWLEDGEMENTS

I should like to thank the following for assistance with this book: Professor Jim Thorpe (Maryland), Bruce Clarke Jnr (Austria), Frau L. Heydrich, Herr Ritter (deceased), Herr W. Trees (Aachen), Herr Morgenschweiss (Aachen) Herr Giskes (deceased), Herr Gorki (Düren), Herr Skorzeny (deceased) and the editors of the *Dürener Zeitung* and *Dürener Nachrichten*.

C.W.

INTRODUCTION

'There's been a change of plan,' the Doctor whispered. He had appeared, totally unexpectedly, at the station a minute before. Although he had arranged the journey for me, and the subsequent meeting, he had not planned to come with me. Now, surprisingly, he had turned up on this cold winter morning. Was it all part of some cat-and-mouse game? Or was it just play-acting? After all the war in the shadows had been over for nearly a quarter of a century now.

Apparently we were not now going to Hamburg, the agreed-upon destination of the day before. Instead we would travel to Harburg on the other side of the River Elbe. I understood, didn't I? The man I was going to interview was still wanted in Germany – or at least he couldn't enter the country legally. We didn't want any trouble with the police, did we? I agreed. We didn't. Besides the 'Reds' – the Doctor still used words like that – would dearly love to get their hands on him. So he had to keep changing his plans constantly. You understand, don't you? Again I understood.

An hour later we were in Harburg. Outside the shabby station a black BMW, which didn't carry the local licence plates, was waiting. The driver, who didn't introduce himself – in itself something strange in very formal West Germany – was big, burly and sullen. I'd soon discover that all those who guarded the man I was coming to see were like that. We were driven around, back and forth up and down the same streets, for some ten minutes before the driver was satisfied that we weren't being tailed. Then he dropped us off at a nondescript flat in Harburg's residential district.

The flat was full of middle-aged men who judging by their accents and their clothes, were not all Germans. Most of them looked wary, if not worried. There was whisky and schnapps a-plenty, and it was disappearing down their gullets very rapidly considering that it was only ten o'clock in the morning.

Finally whoever was in charge decided that everything was

safe. A telephone call was made in another room. Moments later a fleet of cars appeared as if by magic and we were off, one car lagging behind the others to check if we were being followed.

As we drove across the Elbe and headed into Hamburg I learned the reason for the 'great man's' presence in Germany. In Madrid, to where he had escaped from an Allied internment camp in 1948, his doctors had diagnosed a tumour on his spine. It had to be removed, but the operation was tricky. If it went wrong, he could be paralysed for life. His doctors advised him that the best place to have the operation was Germany. Naturally he ran the risk of being arrested, but he was prepared to run that risk, as he had run risks all his life.

Once General Eisenhower, the Allied Supreme Commander, had called him 'the most dangerous man in Europe'. He lay on a hospital bed surrounded by his ex-commandos, who had come from all over Europe to guard their old CO. He was obviously a sick man. He had lost a great deal of weight and his skin had a yellow, unhealthy tinge. But his face, criss-crossed with the sabre scars of his youth, still had that bold challenging look that I remembered from the wartime photos, when his exploits had made him famous.

'Skorzeny,' he said and offered me his hand, even attempting to bow his head a little.

Suddenly I remembered that bitterly cold day in December 1944, when I, with a bunch of other boys in uniform, had been rushed to guard a cross-roads in the Belgian countryside. Behind us we left panic: officers burning secret documents, NCOs breaking bottles of beer and spirits against the wall of the NAAFI, others hastily assembling drafts for the front. Skorzeny's commandos were everywhere, they said. They were dressed as Americans. Everyone was suspect. Shoot first; ask questions afterwards. Now, here was the man who had master-minded that operation, one of the great psychological victories of the Second World War.

Now he faced his last battle. In due course the surgeon was to discover that he had not one but two tumours on his spine, both malignant. For a while he was paralysed from the waist down. 'I thought he would be so discouraged that he'd just give up,' recalled Heinz Wirmer, one of his former SS commandos who had accompanied him from Madrid to the hospital in Hamburg-Boberg. 'He certainly surprised me. Within hours of regaining consciousness, he was hollering for a therapist and vowing that he would walk again.' Which indeed he did and continued to do so for another five years until his death in 1975.

Skorzeny's courage and determination at that time was typical of him and the men he led, the SS commandos and their forerunners, Admiral Canaris's Brandenburgers, who had gone to war even before it had started, four days too early in fact! A mere thousand of them cleared the way for Germany's blitzkrieg westwards in May, 1940. Thereafter they fought and plotted over three continents and in a dozen different countries. They robbed diamonds to sabotage Britian's war effort in South Africa. They tried to raise the flag of revolt in Egypt to the rear of Montgomery's Eighth Army. They made contacts with Welsh and Scottish nationalists and, naturally, with the IRA. When Skorzeny took over ever more drastic and grandiose methods were planned, ones which might have changed the course of history: the murder of the 'Big Three'; the rescue of Mussolini, the kidnapping of the Regent of Hungary to keep that country in the war on Germany's side, to name but three.

For six years the Brandenburgers and the SS Commandos fought their war in the shadows. In a way they were heroes, but they were also victims: abandoned in the Russian wilderness, clubbed to death in the Rumanian mountains or left to die in the Libyan desert. Sometimes one could have wished them a better fate, as for the three pseudo-Americans of Skorzeny's great deception operation in the Ardennes. Sentenced to death as spies by their American captors, they pleaded for mercy: 'We have been captured by the Americans without firing a single shot, because we did not wish to become murderers. We were sentenced to death and we are now dying for criminals who have not only us but also – and what is worse – our families on their conscience.' Their plea didn't help. The three young men were taken out on the morning of 23 December, 1944, placed against a wall and shot. Spying and sabotage is, after all, a dangerous business.

This, then, is the largely unknown story of Hitler's special forces in the Second World War. It was a war fought in the shadows with no quarter given and none expected. It is not a 'nice' story, but in those days, half a century ago now, there were no 'nice' stories.

Charles Whiting, Bleialf, Germany, 1995.

One: Father Christmas Goes to War
1939–40

'My God, if England comes into this, it will be the end of our poor Germany.'

Admiral Canaris, 1 September, 1939.

The decisive order came at eight o'clock on the evening of Thursday, 24 August, 1939. The mysterious Admiral Canaris, known behind his back as 'Father Christmas', due to his shock of snowy-white hair, received it at his headquarters in Berlin's Tirpitzufer. The Führer would march into Poland within the next forty-eight hours. The Admiral was ordered to have sixteen combat teams of his Department Two (Special Operations) ready for action in front of the *Wehrmacht* on the evening of the following day.

The die had been cast. The war could begin. Now the teleprinters started to clatter. Telephones rang. Dispatch riders came and went at speed. Staff officers, with important-looking papers under their arms, hurried to and fro down the echoing corridors of the *Abwehr* (Secret Service) HQ.

Along the country's border with Poland, Canaris's special troops, the Brandenburgers* (named after their garrison town) prepared for action. They were a tough bunch; ethnic Germans from the minorities spread over Eastern Europe from Rumania to Russia, renegade fascist nationalists with German officers and NCOs who preferred adventurous and highly dangerous covert operations to the routine tactics of the regular army.

Mostly they were dressed in Polish uniforms or in rough-and-ready mufti, with the Polish-speakers among them ready to do most of the talking once they had slipped across the frontier. There Teams 'Bisek' and 'Georgey' would smuggle in high

---

* At this time their cover name was 'Special Engineer Battalion 800'. They became the Brandenburg Battalion on 15 October, 1939.

explosives to sabotage key military targets. Another team was going in disguised as Silesian miners. Its task was to prevent the Poles from sabotaging the local mines, soon to be vital to the German war industry.

But the most important mission was given to the team led by Lieutenant Albrecht Herzner, a big, burly man with sandy hair, who was both tough and intelligent; he had gained his doctorate in the thirties before joining the Brandenburgers.

Exactly one year earlier he had been a member of the right-wing resistance team which had planned to assassinate Hitler before he dragged Germany into a new world war. In September, 1938, Herzner and his fellow plotters had been hidden in a number of Berlin apartments ready to assassinate the Führer. But at the last moment Mussolini had called a European conference at which Hitler made some concessions and the threat of imminent war had been averted. Now, unwittingly, Herzner was to be the soldier who fired the first shots of the Second World War in the service of the man he had vowed to gun down twelve months ago.

The Herzner Team had the task of securing the Jablunkov Pass in the Beskids Mountains. Through the pass ran the railway line linking German-occupied Czechoslovakia, via the station at Mosty, to Polish Silesia. It was a pass vital to the German invaders. The plan of attack called for two German panzer divisions to be sent through the pass and race for the Polish city of Cracow. Here they would contain all Polish forces in the area and then drive on for Warsaw with little or no hindrance.

At one o'clock on the morning of Saturday, 26 August, Herzner issued his orders. As a red signal flare rose above the German lines, the Brandenburgers emerged from their hiding places and crossed into Polish territory. Now they began to climb the mountain road. Despite the cold air of the Beskids, their hands were damp with sweat. For they knew what their fate would be if they were taken prisoner by the Poles. As most of them were in civilian clothes or Polish uniforms, they'd be put against the nearest wall and shot out of hand. The Second World War had begun.

But, unknown to Herzner and his Brandenburgers advancing on the first Polish position, where the alert had already been sounded, the war had suddenly been cancelled.

Confusion reigned in Berlin. The day before, Mussolini had

withdrawn from his grandiose 'Pact of Steel' with Germany. He had sent Hitler a letter saying that Italy wouldn't be ready for war until 1942. On the same day Hitler heard from the British and French ambassadors that both their countries would probably fight if the Führer invaded Poland. That night, at six o'clock, Hitler received further bad news. Britain had just signed a treaty with Poland. This transformed the former's hitherto unilateral guarantee of Polish independence into a pact of mutual assistance.

Hitler lost his nerve and called Field Marshal Wilhelm Keitel, head of Army HQ, to the Berlin Chancellery and told him, 'Stop everything at once. I need time for negotiation.'

Keitel recalled his staff to duty. Dozens of calls were made, right down to battalion level. One small unit was caught just before it went into action because its commander stopped to relieve himself for the last time and heard the phone ringing. One minute later and he would have been off.

Then a staff officer remembered the Brandenburgers. A car was sent flying to the HQ of 'Father Christmas'. Luckily Captain Gaedke found the *Abwehr* chief without difficulty. He was resting on the couch in his office. For it was his habit frequently to change the place where he slept to hamper any attempt on his life. As Gaedke came running down the corridor, the Admiral's two dachshunds, which his staff declared he loved more than his two daughters, started barking.

The officer told Canaris that the Führer had called off the invasion of Poland 'on political grounds'; 'You must do everything possible to halt your combat teams.'

The wheels were set in motion at once, while a small group of Canaris's intimate collaborators gathered in his room. He told them: 'The Führer is done for. Hitler will never survive this blow.' His eyes betrayed a sense of joy at the prospect. 'Peace has been saved for the next twenty years.'

But in the general excitement that this might well mean the end of Adolf Hitler, Canaris and his staff officers forgot that no one had been able to contact the Herzner Team. Herzner was going to war all on his own.

His men went into the attack with a will. Most of them had been born in Poland as members of the German minority. They hated the Poles and looked down on them as third class citizens. The fact that the pass was held by a vastly superior number of

Poles didn't worry them. They slammed into the defenders, shouting wildly as they moved forward. Within the hour they had swept the Poles from the mountain road.

Now they advanced on Mosty railway station. Here a mixed bag of border police, soldiers and railway workers had dug themselves in. A fierce fight broke out, but the Brandenburgers attacked with such ferocity that soon white flags made from tableclothes started to flutter from the outbuildings. Finally a middle-aged Polish colonel came out with his hands above his head. He wanted to surrender.

But Herzner was puzzled. Where was the link-up? Surely the first armoured reconnaissance cars should be here by now. He turned to the Polish colonel. 'What's the matter? Aren't Germany and Poland at war?'

The Pole shrugged. 'I've already told you they aren't. You can find it out for yourself if you don't believe me'.

'How?'

'By calling your base on the telephone.'

Remarkably, the civilian telephone network still functioned. After some delay Herzner managed to get through to his HQ at the Slovakian town of Zilina. The frantic Divisional Intelligence Officer who had been trying to reach Harzner for hours bellowed, 'Retreat at once.' He was to leave behind any prisoners and whatever booty had been taken. 'Get back over the frontier at once,' he cried.

But it was already too late. Lieutenant Herzner who was to die mysteriously two years later, had already won his little place in history. He had fired the first shots of the war to come. With his seventy-five men he had taken 1,200 Poles prisoner. Now the Poles knew what to expect from the Germans.*

2

Admiral Canaris was forty-seven when, in 1935, he was summoned to Berlin to take over command of the German Secret Service, the *Abwehr*. But, with his wrinkled, sallow skin and

---

* When Canaris recommended Harzner for the Iron Cross he was told by Keitel that he couldn't have it as it could only be awarded in time of war. Harzner did win it later on.

white hair, he looked much older. Indeed his staff instantly called him '*der Alte*' (the old one) behind his back. Himmler and Heydrich, the man responsible for the SS's intelligence and secret police service, were not so complimentary. They named him '*der Weihnachtsmann*' – 'Father Christmas'.

Canaris, who had an adventurous career in naval raiders, spying and right-wing putsches behind him, threw himself into his work with tremendous energy. Up to now the *Abwehr* had been '*ein kleiner Laden*' (a small shop). Now, with the limitless funds that the new Nazi government had for all things military, Canaris was in a position to expand his service rapidly.

In essence he reorganized the *Abwehr* into three departments: Group I, military intelligence, Group II, military sabotage and Group III, counter espionage.

Under the command of Colonel Lahousen, Group II started to recruit agents all over Europe, who, directed by German officers, would carry out acts of sabotage, political assassination and armed insurrection all over the world. From Bombay to Brussels resourceful young men were enlisted into the ranks of the fighting arm of this organization, the Special Engineer Battalion 800, later called the *Regiment Brandenburg*. They were IRA killers, Dutch fascists, Boer fundamentalists, Egyptian undercover revolutionaries, Russian nationalists, even a few Jewish freedom fighters who believed that by supporting Hitler they might ensure that Palestine, the future Israel, would be allowed to accept, against British and Arab wishes, a flood of Jewish settlers who would make up the new Jewish state.

Now the restless *Abwehr* chief, of whom his staff said he had no '*Sitzfleisch*' (literally 'sitting flesh'), who travelled Europe constantly under a variety of false names and identities, was in a position to 'take out' Germany's enemies without recourse to the due legal process. German socialist propagandists in Prague were murdered in their homes, communists in Denmark and Sweden were blackmailed into returning to their homeland, other German dissenters in France and Belgium were quietly liquidated. Slowly, as Germany prepared for war, Canaris developed a new kind of force, which would be the model for all future special forces: brave ruthless men, who could lie in deep cover for a long time, self-reliant and self-sufficient, who in small groups efficiently carried out tasks that would have been impossible for larger groups. The concept of the commando had been born.

Now the little Admiral, of whom William Shirer has written, 'He was so shadowy a figure that no two writers agree as to what kind of man he was, or what he believed in, if anything much,' performed an astonishing *volte-face*. The year before, in 1938, he had been privy to the generals' plot to kill Hitler, in which Herzner might have fired the murder weapon. Yet, six days after the Herzner mission to Poland, he assembled his staff and briefed them on what it meant now that Hitler had at last gone to war with Poland. He began by reminding his officers that they belonged to the 'silent service'. They had to refrain from telling the world about their exploits. 'I demand unquestioning and unconditional positive loyalty to the Führer.'

He finished his little pep talk with a 'Heil Hitler' and the German salute. They clicked to attention as he left and made his way through the dimly lit corridors of his Tirpitzufer HQ. (Always cost-conscious, Canaris insisted that electricity be saved wherever possible; hence the poorly lit rooms and corridors.)

On his way to his office he bumped into the gigantic ex-Gestapo man and now anti-Nazi, Dr Gisevius. He told Canaris, 'It has just been reported that England has ordered total mobilization.'

Canaris drew him to one side and performed the so-called 'German look', a quick glance over the shoulder to left and right to check whether they were being overheard. He knew what this meant. He had always told his staff that if England entered a war, America would follow; and he feared America's military and industrial potential above all things. 'My God,' he said, 'if England comes into this, it will be the end of our poor Germany!'

But there was no time to reflect upon that particular bit of bad news. Canaris had to follow the troops into Poland and observe the work of his Brandenburgers. What he saw took the edge off Germany's victories. Several of his men in the field told him of the systematic murder of both Poles and Jews in the course of the *Wehrmacht*'s march into the heart of Poland. *Reichsführer SS* Himmler's murder squads, for instance, were carrying out the wholesale slaughter of the Polish intelligentsia, apparently on the orders of the Führer himself.

Canaris met Hitler's special train in the sidings of the little Polish town of Ilnau on 12 September, 1939. Accompanied by the chief of the Brandenburgers, Colonel Lahousen, he approached Keitel first, telling him what he had learned of these mass murders. 'I have information, *Herr Generaloberst*, that mass executions are being planned in Poland. In particular, the nobility and clergy are to be exterminated.' Then Canaris added a word of warning: 'The world will hold the Army responsible for these actions being carried out before our eyes.'

Keitel replied coldly, 'If I were you, Herr Canaris, I would not get mixed up in this business. The Führer has already decided on this question. He has already informed the Commander-in-Chief that, if the Army does not want to have anything to do with this matter, then the SS and Gestapo will take care of it. For that reason each military commander will have a civilian appointed to his command who will be responsible for racial extermination.'

Before Canaris could protest any more, Hitler himself appeared and engaged the Admiral in intelligence questions on France's intentions in the West.

In later years the various biographers of Admiral Canaris regarded that meeting in the train, in which Canaris finally saw just how heartless and cruel Hitler was, as the turning point in the Admiral's career. From now on he would be firmly in the camp of the anti-Hitler conspirators. Canaris's earliest biographer, a member of his own service, Dr Abshagen, maintains that 'he was deeply moved by the events in Poland'. One of the latest, Ladislas Farago, also says that '[Canaris] was stunned, mortified, scandalized,' and that 'he was emotionally convulsed and physically sick when he got back to Berlin on the fourteenth. It was not his habit to put down on paper anything unpleasant or controversial for fear that this record might come back to harm him. But this time he sat down immediately upon his return and prepared the minutes of the conference.' Thereafter 'Canaris never recovered from the shock of the experience.'

But his own diary contains no record of his 'shock'. Instead, as Germany moved from victory to victory in the eighteen-day-long campaign in Poland, Canaris seemed carried away with a kind of triumphant euphoria. Day after day that September he and his jubilant staff officers planned yet another blow against Britain and the British Empire. For Canaris saw the British as Germany's main opponent.

As he saw it, the 'oppressed' peoples of the British Empire were only waiting for the signal to rise. With German gold and the leadership of a handful of bold Brandenburgers, they would rise in revolt from Bombay to Belfast. In the First World War

Germany had had some success in the Middle East and Southern Ireland. Now Germany would act on a much grander scale.

Canaris already had links with the IRA. Jim O'Donovan, code-named 'Hero', an IRA bomber, was already being trained in Germany. He and Sean Russell, the IRA's chief-of-staff, who had fled to America, would return to Ireland, together with picked Brandenburgers, to raise the flag of revolution in Ulster.

Canaris had also made approaches to Scottish and Welsh nationalists who wanted to be rid of the English tyranny. Nothing much happened in Scotland, but in Wales Canaris was to have more success. By the start of the German *Luftwaffe*'s bombing campaign against Britain in 1940 Welsh nationalists were lighting huge signal arrows in the hills. These, pointing in the direction of Liverpool and Merseyside, acted as directional beacons for German bombers coming in from the Irish Sea. These signal fires became such a thorn in the authorities' flesh that they sent in troops to winkle the nationalists out. So nothing much came of Canaris's plan to drop Brandenburgers into Wales.*

Brandenburgers were to be sent to Persia to stir up the tribes there against the British and deny them the vital Persian oil. Similar plans were afoot for neighbouring Iraq, where the British controlled the country from a great air base not far from the capital. Soon captured Indian soldiers would be training under the Brandenburgers so that they could parachute into their native country and raise an insurrection against the Raj. Throughout Africa Brandenburgers would soon be undermining the 8th Army in Egypt and sabotaging and destroying the South African diamond and gold mines. They even had contacts with the Jewish underground in British-occupied Palestine, aiding the Haganah in its attempts to throw out the British and turn Palestine into a Jewish homeland, this at a time when Canaris already knew of the shocking treatment of Jews in Germany and Poland. Strange bed-fellows indeed.†

But as 1939 gave way to 1940, Canaris had to put to one side

---

* Some agents were dropped to aid a Welsh national organization which didn't exist. They dropped right into the clutches of the organization's leader, a Welsh police inspector!

† It is often forgotten that Heydrich and Eichmann, authors of the 'Final Solution' already had contact with the Jewish underground before the war. Indeed Eichman spent several months in Palestine, learning some Hebrew and Yiddish in the process.

such plans as a Brandenburger drop into Tibet and another in Thailand. For, as the Phoney War in the West dragged on with the British and the French making no attempt to attack, Hitler decided he would take the offensive.

Again the Brandenburgers would be needed to achieve surprise on Germany's frontiers with Holland, Belgium, Luxembourg and Northern France. By bold *coups de main*, Hitler wanted the Brandenburgers to open the way for the mass of the *Wehrmacht*. Somehow means must be found of breaking through the Dutch border canal-and-river defensive system and the rugged hills of the Belgian-Luxembourg frontier area before France and Britain could rush up troops to defend these positions. In essence, the handful of Brandenburgers were being asked to capture these key positions by any means possible so that the *Wehrmacht* could fight the decisive battle of the war in the West on the flat plains of Northern France. The great German victory in the West depended upon less than one thousand men.

3

By early 1940 Canaris's agents were travelling the length and breadth of the frontier region in the Benelux countries. They photographed and sketched the details of the bridges at Maastricht, Gennep and that bridge which in four years would become the most famous in the world, the bridge at Arnhem. They reconnoitred the country roads through the Ardennes to the bridges over the River Meuse and they noted all the details of the Luxembourg Grand Ducal Family in that city and the exit roads leading south to France some eighteen miles away.

Other agents were busy in second-hand and pawn shops in Liège, Antwerp and Brussels buying up second-hand gendarme and military uniforms. Here the Brandenburgers suffered an annoying set-back. One of the agents buying uniforms was captured in Antwerp with the uniforms in his possession. When it was discovered he was a German, questions were asked. A Flemish language paper published a caricature of Goering wearing the uniform of a Belgian tram conductor (the marshal had an obsession with uniforms and changed his as many as sixteen times a day) and admiring himself in the mirror. The caption read: 'This *does* suit me well!'

In Berlin Canaris's staff waited tensely to see what the Dutch and Belgian authorities would do. For they knew that the fate of the German parachute division to be dropped around Rotterdam depended upon a swift link-up with the ground troops crossing the bridges into Holland. Would the Dutch reinforce their border troops? In the event they didn't. Neither did the Belgians, which was very surprising, especially as a top staff officer in Canaris's outfit was feeding them information about the coming invasion.

Another group of agents was now sent out to discover where the Dutch royal family, government and high command would take up their quarters in the event of war. Under the command of Captain Walter Schulze-Bernett, who boasted that he'd find them 'because in Holland there is no stone we don't know about,' they set off on their mission. Once the attack had started, Brandenburg paratroopers would be dropped to capture all prominent people. They would then be pawns in Hitler's hands, thus bringing the war in Holland to a speedy end.

At the southern end of the German attack line, at the little military airfield outside the Eifel township of Bitburg, a fleet of Fieseler Storch light observation aircraft was being assembled. Each plane could carry two men in addition to the pilot. A unit of Brandenburgers was being readied to take part in what could only be termed as an aerial kidnapping. When the attack started they would fly across the German border with Luxembourg and set up road blocks on the exit routes from the capital. It would be their mission to capture the fleeing Grand Ducal family and another country would be blackmailed into surrender.

By the middle of April Canaris's staff officers were working all out to complete the planning of half a dozen covert operations, all of which had to receive the personal approval of the Führer. In all Colonel Lahousen, Head of Group II, had one thousand men at his disposal, two hundred of whom were Dutch fascist renegades under the command of the Dutch fascist leader, Herdtmann.*

About twenty of these men, all Dutch speakers, would be dropped with General Student's 7th Parachute Division over the north-western part of Holland. It would the Brandenburgers' job

* By the time the war ended one in five of German defenders of Graebbe Line in Holland was Dutch.

16

to assist the paratroopers in any way they could and also to apprehend the Dutch Royal Family. Five hundred Brandenburgers were attached to the German Sixth Army. It would be their task to seize the bridges across the Albert Canal, the Meuse and the Rhine. Another two hundred were seconded to the German Fourth Army for similar duties in the Ardennes in Southern Belgium, while the remainder had the job of capturing key installations in Luxembourg and Northern France and, if possible, seize the Grand Ducal family. These Brandenburgers would dress in German uniform and be flown in in the light Fieseler Storch aircraft.

By the first week of May, 1940, all Canaris's plans had been approved by the Führer. Now his Brandenburgers, taking with them the Belgian and Dutch uniforms they would wear to fool their enemies, started to move to the frontiers with Belgium, Holland and Luxembourg. Behind them massed a huge German army, much of it armoured, ready to launch what the shocked Western allies would be soon calling *the Blitzkrieg* – the lightning war – a new kind of warfare in which armoured forces moved forward, striking their opponents when they could or simply just outflanking enemy strongpoints. It was the same tactics the *Wehrmacht* would be using four years later during the Battle of the Bulge. And again in 1944 the Brandenburgers and their successors would pave the way for these long-range armoured thrusts by trickery and deceit. There was one catch, however. *The American enemy knew the Brandenburgers were coming!*

Back in April, 1940, Colonel Oster, a key member of the *Abwehr*, had asked Colonel Sas, the Dutch military attaché in Berlin, to his home for a chat. When his guest was settled, Oster, one of the leaders of the anti-Hitler group within the *Abwehr*, said, 'I've asked you to come here because you are an old friend of mine and I have an important communication to make to you.'

'About Holland?' Sas asked him.

'No, not about Holland,' Oster said, 'or shall we say, not yet Holland. This time it's about Denmark and Norway.' Oster then gave Sas the full details of Hitler's plan to invade the Nordic countries which Sas promptly passed on to the Danish ambassador. Thus for the first time Oster betrayed his country, not for reward, but in order to undermine Hitler, whom he hated passionately.

17

Unfortunately for Holland, Sas's superior, the Dutch Commander-in-Chief, General Winkelmann, did not have much faith in a man who was prepared to betray his country to a potential enemy and decided to disregard Sas's information.

On Friday, 3 May Oster told Sas that there was a definite possibility that Holland would soon be invaded and added, 'You have had so much difficulty with your people. They won't believe you anyway.'

On the following Thursday the two men met again for dinner and Oster said 'My dear Sas, this really is it. The orders [to invade Holland] have not been countermanded and that swine has actually gone to the front. This is the end. I hope we shall see each other after the war.'

Sas hurried away to inform his colleague, the Belgian military attaché. Then he called the Dutch War Office. He recognized the voice at the other end. As he reported after the war, 'Lieutenant, you recognize my voice. I am Sas, military attaché in Berlin. Listen to me carefully. Tomorrow morning at dawn hold fast. Do you understand me? Repeat what I have said, please.'

The young officer did so and added, 'That means letter 210 received.'

This was a code the Dutch had agreed upon. Letter 200 meant the invasion of Holland. The added 10 was the date.

But at the Dutch War Office they still didn't quite believe Sas. Late that night he was roused from his bed by a call from the chief of Dutch military intelligence. His every word expressed doubt. He said, 'I am sorry to have received such bad news about the operation on your wife. Have you consulted all the available specialists?'

Sas grew angry at having to use an open telephone line for the second time that night. He snapped, 'Yes I have. I can't understand why you are bothering me at such a moment. The operation is taking place tomorrow morning at dawn.' Then he slammed the phone down. Then, sadly, Colonel Sas collected his pyjamas and toothbrush and went over to the Dutch embassy. Tomorrow morning, he was sure, the Gestapo would come to arrest him and his fellow diplomats. He had done his duty. But would those dolts in the Hague take any notice of his warning?

Dawn, 10 May, 1940. On this Friday the course of European history would be changed and for six hours the handful of

18

Brandenburger volunteers would be the key to that earth-shaking change. In the early dawn light the Dutch guards at the bridges at Arnhem and Maastricht saw what they took to be parties of German deserters being escorted by guards dressed in Dutch uniform. But, the defenders asked, why so many deserters and why hadn't Germany's own frontier police stopped them? Then a flare sailed into the sky, colouring the faces of those below. A challenge rang out. Suddenly the guards and 'prisoners' were doubling, firing from the hip as they ran. A fire-fight broke out. The Dutch had been alerted after all.

At Nijmegen Captain Flecke's Brandenburgers fought it out with the Dutch, men of an army which hadn't fought a European war since the time of Napoleon. But the Dutchmen gave as good as they got. They inflicted heavy casualties on the Brandenburgers, but in the end the Dutch soldiers began to pull back. The Brandenburgers renewed their efforts. Suddenly the bridge blew up with a great roar. A moment later the other bridge at Nijmegen also blew up. The Brandenburgers had failed.

The surprise attack on Arnhem also failed, but, as the German army started to pile up on the other side of the frontier waiting for emergency bridges to be thrown across the rivers by engineers, the Brandenburgers were successful.

At the bridge at Gennep the team under the command of Lieutenant Walter went into action well before dawn. Some of them were disguised as prisoners, but prisoners with special machine pistols and stick grenades hidden beneath their greatcoats. They were guarded by the Dutch fascist renegades dressed in the impressive blue uniform of Dutch military policemen. Before the Dutch defenders could react, they were across, cutting the wires to the detonation chamber beneath the bridge, rounding up the guards and firing on the advancing Dutch troops. But it was already too late for the Dutch infantry. The first tanks were beginning to clatter across the bridge. Soon General von Reichenau would switch his stalled 6th Army from Maastricht to Gennep. The German paratroops, nearly a hundred miles away, would be saved.

As Dr Leverkuehn, who was himself part of Canaris's service, would comment long afterwards, 'The gaining of a purely military objective by Secret Service methods, in other words the tactical co-ordination of the action of regular troops and agents, was successfully employed for the first time in this Gennep affair.'

In Belgium the Brandenburgers seized all their objectives and were soon accompanying the German 3rd Army in its dash through the Ardennes, helping to capture strongpoints and cutting communications. Above all they spread rumours of German parachutist agents and spies being abroad everywhere. Something akin to panic struck Belgium. Masses of people took to the roads, heading for the south. Suddenly the British Expeditionary Force and their French allies, heading into Belgium to stop the Germans before they reached the plains of Flanders and Northern France, were hindered, even halted, by streams of panic-stricken civilians.

There was wild talk of nuns with hairy legs being dropped by parachute and orders were issued as to how to strip a nun and find the telltale marks of parachute harness. Police officers hurried to every shop selling a popular substitute coffee made from chicory called pacha. They ordered the bemused shopkeeper to remove the 'pacha' sales sign immediately. As Belgian hotel worker Lars Moen remembered, this was because 'the Germans had put on the back of them indications useful to parachutists landing in the locality. Thanks to this arrangement, a German parachutist needed to carry on his person no incriminating maps and addresses. Wherever he might land all he needed to find was the nearest 'Pacha' chicory sign. On its back he would find cryptic indications giving him the location of the nearest German agent and how to find him.'

That May panic was in the very air in Belgium. It was no different in Luxembourg. Although the Luxembourgers spoke a German dialect and had many contacts with the local Germans on the other side of the frontier, no love was lost between them and the Germans. But they couldn't fight back as their army numbered fewer than a hundred men. The richer citizens headed south for France. With them went Grand Duke Felix with his wife and children.

Unknown to the Grand Duke, the fleet of Fieseler Storchs carrying the Brandenburgers had already crossed the Luxembourg frontier. Now the fleet of small aircraft flew at tree-top height from Echternach on the border towards the city. When the lead pilot spotted the spires of Luxembourg's Notre Dame cathedral he veered to the south and he and his fellow pilots began putting their planes down near the roads which led to Esch-sur-Sure, the great border steel and mining town.

But they were too late. The Grand Duke's car had already sped into France and he was safe. It would be four years before he would return as a British brigadier, unable to find his tiny principality and moaning because the departing Germans hadn't taken the ponderous palace furniture with them. 'I had rather hoped,' he told his American escort, 'that the Boches would take all of these. However, my wife will be happy.'

So the Brandenburgers had yet another failure. But on the whole their successes had outweighed their failure. On 14 May their commander was called to Hitler's HQ. As he wrote to Canaris later, 'Our efforts at the start of the operations have been marked by high regard here.' With effect from 15 May the battalion was to be increased to regimental strength and called 'Training Regiment Brandenburg for Special Duties'. Later it was announced that two-thirds of the participants in the dawn attack of five days before were to be awarded the Iron Cross.

But there was one fly in the ointment for Canaris. The German secret listening service, which tapped all foreign calls, had picked up Colonel Sas's two calls on 9 May. It hadn't taken long for the experts to find out that the figure '210' mentioned by Sas was a coded signal indicating that Holland was to be invaded on May 10. Another call to Brussels from Belgium's minister to the Vatican had also shown that he had known the attack on his country was coming. Who had told the Dutch military attaché and the Belgian ambassador? It was clear that it could only be a high-ranking German staff officer.

As soon as Canaris received 'the brown bird', as the listening service's reports were called because they were printed on brown paper, he knew that the traitor had to be Oster. What was he to do? There were too many officers in the *Abwehr* like Oster, men who had been deeply involved in the plot to kill Hitler two years before. If he ordered an inquiry, he could well be implicated himself and he knew Hitler would show no mercy.

But his arch rival for the control of Germany's whole intelligence *apparat* had also been ordered by the Führer to find the traitor immediately. 'The man with the iron heart,' as the Führer called him, had entered the picture.

Two: The Man with the Iron Heart
1940–41

'He frightens me. He is a man with a heart of iron.'

Adolf Hitler, 1940

Reinhard Tristan Heydrich, the head of the SS's police *apparat*, had had a chip on his shoulder since his earliest years. As a boy, he had been an outsider. He was handicapped by a high-pitched falsetto voice and fat girlish hips. He also played the violin. It was not surprising, therefore, that his schoolmates, cruel as all children can be, made fun of him. If that was not enough, Heydrich thought he was Jewish, as did his schoolmates.

Soon this blond, blue-eyed son of a musician realized that, if he was not to remain a worm for the rest of his life, he would have to be crueller, bolder, and more powerful than the rest of the 'mob'. Deliberately he set out to toughen himself up and to stand out as a superior individual in the eyes of his contemporaries. He took to walking aggressively to school with one foot in the curb and one in the gutter. He never deflected from his course, even when adults got in his way. Anyone who tried to push him aside got punched. Then he would throw himself at his opponent, however big, with a reckless courage that bordered on mania. He started showing off to the boys who had once mocked him. Once he climbed on to the school roof during lessons and, in full view of the horrified staff and students, walked along the edge of the gutter, with a hundred foot drop below.

Later, as a cadet in the German Navy in the late '20s, he transferred his aggressiveness to fencing, becoming a German champion, and to the relentless pursuit of women. He was not too particular in his choice. In latter days he often boasted he had had them all – 'white, yellow, brown, black' – they were all the same to him – '*cunts*'. He took them by force or with hard cash. But eventually his womanizing caught up with him. In 1931 he was court-martialled and kicked out of the Navy because of an unsavoury affair with a naval officer's daughter.

In the depressed Germany of 1931, with six million men unemployed, there were few job opportunities for a disgraced naval signals officer. He was offered a post as a glider pilot instructor, but, on the advice of his new wife, he turned it down. Instead he applied to join the SS and travelled to Munich to meet the head of the Nazi organization. Heinrich Himmler thought Heydrich had been an intelligence officer in the Navy (the words for 'signals' and 'intelligence' are the same in German). He gave Heydrich pen and paper and allowed him twenty minutes to draw up a plan for an SS counter-intelligence service. Heydrich, of course, knew nothing of such matters, but he had always been an avid reader of novels about the English Secret Service. Using these as a base, he drew up the required plan, which so impressed Himmler that he was accepted into the SS.

Now Heydrich embarked upon what was to prove an amazing career. With the fervour and energy of the newly converted, he organized the Nazi Security Service, a combination of the secret police and the SS's secret service. he turned it into a rigidly efficient outfit which became the terror of the régime's enemies. But not only his enemies feared him, the Nazis did too. Himmler called him 'the living card index, a brain which held all the threads and wove them all together'. By 1939 he was an SS general, described by Hitler as 'the man with the iron heart'.

But in spite of his power and his overwhelming ambition, there was something pathological in the way Heydrich tried to keep to himself. When Himmler offered him the '*du*', ie asked him to use the familiar 'thou' form of address instead of the formal 'you', Heydrich asked his boss not to 'force this great honour on him'. He lived modestly and ordered his wife to do the same. Their only regular guests were Admiral Canaris and his wife, the men being linked by their secret service activities and their former service in the German Navy.

When he was drunk, which was often, a fierce temper would break the normal icy surface. Then he'd tour the brothels of Berlin with his cronies, taking women by force, not even paying the whores for their services, and no one dared to ask him for money. Once, after a long-drawn-out drinking session, he staggered to a mirror, looked at his face and cried, 'Just look at his nose, his face – typical Jewish! A Jewish lout!' On another occasion he stormed into his bathroom and drew his revolver, crying, 'Now at last I've got you, scum!' Then he pumped two shots into the mirror.

But when he was sober Heydrich was cool, cruel and calculating. This exaggerated feeling of belonging yet not belonging because he thought he was Jewish made him a fearsome technocrat of death. He didn't believe in the Hitler myth. Nor did he subscribe to Himmler's absurd racial theories. He was motivated solely by expediency and his own burning ambition. He once confessed to some cronies that he would be the first to do away with Hitler, 'if the old man makes a mess of things'.

Now it was given to Heydrich to prove that the leak about the offensive in the West had come from Canaris's *Abwehr*. It was a task that attracted him. Yet at the same time he knew he had to act very carefully. If he could prove his case it might well mean Canaris's dismissal and, then slowly but surely, he could extend the power of his own *apparat* over military intelligence. But Canaris had the protection of the War Office and the War Office had the ear of Field Marshal Keitel, who was the Führer's chief adviser. One wrong step and he might find himself being dismissed. After all, in the eyes of the War Office's intelligence experts, he was a cashiered ex-naval officer who hadn't the years of professional training that they had received.

Heydrich did his best, but he faced grave difficulties. While Canaris had moles in Heydrich's office, he had none in the *Abwehr*. Nor could his Gestapo arrest *Abwehr* agents or officers of the *Wehrmacht*. The *Abwehr* could issue passports, give Jews a document indicating that they were Aryan, transfer currency abroad. In other words, the *Abwehr* was a world of its own, one which it was very difficult to penetrate.

Nevertheless Heydrich began compiling a list of suspects, including Colonel Oster. But Canaris was determined to protect his organization and his career. Boldly he claimed that he had been the source of the leak. It had been a feint to confuse the enemy as to where the attack would really come. The explanation was accepted by the Führer and the matter went no further.

Heydrich felt frustrated, but he continued to add the names of *Abwehr* officers whom he felt were disloyal or traitorous to what he called his 'ammunition pack', which would be used to give Canaris and his men the *coup de grace* when the time was ripe. As he told his SS cronies, 'I'll bury old Father Christmas yet'.

But two years later it was to be old Father Christmas who would help to bury Heydrich after his assassination by Czech patriots in Prague. It was said that Canaris wept at the funeral. But the 'ammunition pack' remained intact, being added to over the years until the time came to use it against Canaris.

2

On 26 June, 1940, Hitler ventured as close to Britain as he ever would go. He drove to Dunkirk. From the beaches from which the British had fled only three weeks earlier, he surveyed the smudge on the horizon – England. All around him lay the signs of Britain's defeat, burnt-out trucks, shattered bren-gun carriers, the twisted skeletons of wrecked boats in the water. Yet Churchill, the new British Prime Minister, had stubbornly refused to come to terms. Obviously the cigar-smoking old sot was preparing to fight on even though he didn't have a chance.

Originally Hitler had not envisaged an invasion of the British mainland. Now he started to toy with the idea. Knock out Britain and America would be easily dissuaded from entering the war on Britain's side. They would have no base from which to fight in Europe.

Soon after his return to Berlin, Hitler told *Grossadmiral* Raeder, head of the German Navy, of his intentions. Next day Canaris was informed. As the *Abwehr* diary recorded: 'Upon orders of the Chief, operations of the *Abwehr* will henceforth be concentrated on the war with England.'*

Now, with the leak satisfactorily swept under the carpet, Canaris set about his new task. For Lahousen's Brandenburgers it meant preparations for parachute and sabotage operations in the UK, but also much larger operations elsewhere, which Canaris hoped would threaten Britain's life-lines. In particular, the Brandenburgers started to concentrate on 'Operation Felix'.

This was the brainchild of Admiral Canaris himself. He spoke fluent Spanish, was a close acquaintance of the Spanish dictator Franco and thought that 'Felix', the attack on the British fortress

---

* 100 Brandenburgers, all English-speaking, did train that summer to capture Weymouth. The idea was they would draw off forces defending Plymouth and Portsmouth which would then be attacked by regular German troops.

of Gibraltar, would bring Spain in on Germany's side. They would participate in the attack on the Rock and would be rewarded by its return to them. At the same time Britain's most powerful naval base in the Western Mediterranean would be knocked. This would have a decisive influence on Britain's influence in the Middle East and the war that Britain was now fighting in Libya against Germany's ally Italy.

In the first week of July, 1940, Canaris called to his office a brave young officer who had played a great role in the surprise attacks on the Belgian frontier. His company, now expanded to battalion strength, had won over one hundred decorations for bravery in its half-day battle. Captain Hans-Jurgen Rudloff was now ordered to go to Spain and reconnoitre the defences of Gibraltar. As Canaris saw it at the time, Rudloff's battalion would be secretly transported across Spain, while at the same time engineers and artillery would sail from the newly captured French ports to meet up with the Brandenburgers off Gibraltar. When the artillery started their bombardments, the Brandenburgers would rush the Rock, followed by the engineers. They'd take the Rock by surprise.

Rudloff wasn't too impressed by the hasty plan, but orders were orders and the prospect of time in summery southern Spain was tempting.

Canaris followed Rudloff to Spain some time later and sought an audience with Franco. The latter seemed to like the idea, but he didn't think that Spain was ready for war. However, he did grant Canaris all the facilities he needed to spy upon the fortress, even having Spanish Foreign Legion uniforms delivered to the Brandenburgers so that they wouldn't stick out when they entered supposedly neutral Spain.

But as the weeks passed Franco doggedly refused to enter the war on Germany's side. Vichy France tried to show him, with German prompting, just how weak the Rock was. They maintained, correctly, that there were only three Fairey float planes for use in Gibraltar's defence.

Exactly a year after France and Britain had entered the war as allies, a French strike force under the command of the future French Admiral Laine attacked Gibraltar with sixty-four bombers escorted by thirty-six fighters. Their main target was the battle cruiser *Repulse*. But it escaped out to sea, firing every gun as it did so. Laine's attack and the one which followed achieved little.

Still it showed the Spaniards how ill-prepared Gibraltar was for an airborne attack, or even an invasion.

Now Hitler became most enthusiastic about Operation Felix and decided to put more pressure on Franco. A meeting was arranged and the two met at Hendaye on the Spanish frontier on 23 October, 1940. But the meeting ended in failure. The Caudillo was firm. Spain wouldn't be ready for war for another two years and he could allow no attack on the Rock. It was a question of Spain's honour. Later an exhausted Hitler said that he'd rather 'have four teeth pulled out than face another confrontation with the Caudillo'.

When Canaris heard the result, he realized that Franco would never go to war on Germany's side. The risks were too great. So Operation Felix was cancelled.

3

When, in early 1941, Major Ritter of the *Abwehr*'s Hamburg branch first suggested the next plan, called 'Operation Condor', to Admiral Canaris, the latter snapped, 'That's a crazy idea.' He looked at Ritter as if to say, 'My dear Ritter, you can't be altogether right in the head.'

Ritter, who had been running agents into Britain since 1938 and whose cover had now been blown, desperately wanted a new mission in a totally different threatre. So now he suggested 'Condor' to the Admiral.

Four weeks later, however, Canaris, telephoned Ritter, a good English speaker who had spent ten years in the States, and told him he had changed his mind. He could go ahead with his plan, one that might change the course of the war in the Western Desert. It had first been conceived when Ritter met Count Laszlo von Almaszy in Hungary. Almaszy had spent many years of his life exploring the Western Desert. As he had told Ritter at their first meeting, 'Once I'm out of it [the desert], I never want to go back to that burning hell, with no water and no whisky. But after a few weeks in Cairo, I'm always ready to go in once more, to get away from people and face up to its challenges.'

During his years in Cairo he had got to know every Egyptian of any importance. Now, bitter that the British had kicked him out as an enemy alien with only a few hours' notice, he suggested that Germany should secure the services of those Egyptian soldiers who were actively planning to throw the English out of their country, now that Rommel was having such success in the Western Desert.

In particular he drew Ritter's attention to the ex-chief-of-staff of the Egyptian Army, El Masri Pasha, who had been dismissed from his command by the British the previous December for having revealed to the Italians the whole defence plan of the Nile Delta. Now the ageing general had gone over to the young hotheads of the Moslem Brotherhood, such as Captain Gamal Abdel Nasser, who had been impressed by the Nazis when he had represented his country as a weight-lifter at the 1936 Olympics, and Anwar El Sadat, both of whom in the post-war years would become head of an independent Egypt.

During that initial conversation Almaszy had proposed that he and Ritter, with the help of a handful of Brandenburgers, should smuggle El Masri Pasha out of Egypt and into Libya. There he could be used as a tool to cause confusion behind the Eighth Army lines in the Western Desert and perhaps even bring out the whole of the Egyptian Army in revolt. Then Rommel would be able to walk into Cairo with hardly a fight.

Ritter asked, 'Do you really think that we could get the General to work with us against the British?'

'Naturally,' the Count replied. 'I'm convinced he would do it. I've often considered the possibility. But before I met you I couldn't think of anyone to whom I could suggest the idea.'

Then with Canaris's backing, the two plotters, plus a dozen picked Brandenburgers, most of whom spoke fluent English, flew out to Derna in Africa in early March, 1941. There they set about trying to get the General out, but they were dogged by bad luck. They tried first with a submarine, but the coastal waters were too shallow. The next attempt was by aircraft, but when El Masri Pasha's car was delayed the young pilot panicked and flew off without him.

Ritter flew back to Berlin to confer with Canaris. The Admiral was still 'Feuer und Flamme' (fire and flame) for the project, as Ritter remembered, and he gave him a second go-ahead. Then suddenly he frowned and said, 'Watch out for the SD down there.' He was referring to Heydrich's own spy service. A moment later he added a few more words the meaning of which Ritter would only understand much later. He said, 'In peacetime, my dear Ritter, one can overthrow a government when one is dissatisfied with it. But when one attempts to do that kind of thing in wartime then that is treachery to one's own people.'

And with that enigmatic statement, the only one of a political nature that Ritter had ever heard cross the Admiral's lips, they parted. Ritter never saw Canaris again.

When he returned to Derna bad news was awaiting him. Over a drink in the officers' club, the chain-smoking Almaszy told him that he had penetrated far into the desert to a rendezvous point with El Masri Pasha, who, it had been planned, should escape from his English guards and run to a waiting escape plane. But the General had not appeared at the rendezvous at a feature known as the Red Djebel. Next day they knew why. The Egyptian Press reported briefly that the General had been arrested by the British authorities. No further details were given. Again an *Abwehr* plan had ended in failure.

Now it was decided to run in two trained Brandenburgers by plane to a point close to the Egyptian frontier where there was a landing strip in the desert. These two men, one very tall, the other short and plump, were codenamed 'Pat and Patichon' after two Danish film comedians whose appearance they aped. The two Brandenburgers were to make their way to the Egyptian frontier after landing and head for Cairo. Here they would set up a liaison post with the young Egyptian Army officers grouped around Nasser and report back to Rommel's HQ.

This time Ritter wanted no slip-ups and decided to accompany Pat and Patichon to the drop zone. Little did he realize how fatal was this decision, one that would end his five-year career with the *Abwehr*. But, as he rationalized many years after the war, 'In the end it probably saved my neck. I would probably have shared the same fate as Canaris if I had stayed in the organization.'

They set off on a moonlit night and soon arrived over the site. The pilot started to throttle back. The flaps came down. Ritter held on tight. The young pilot didn't seem too sure of himself. He jerked back the stick and the plane's nose rose sharply.

'What in the devil's name are you about, man?' Ritter yelled.

'I can't do it,' he said. 'There are big boulders down there.'

'They're not boulders, just small rocks,' Ritter answered.

But it was already too late. The pilot had turned back and was heading for base. While Ritter fumed, considering half a dozen fearsome punishments for the frightened young pilot, the Heinkel's radio crackled into life. 'Don't land here,' the controller cried, 'we're being bombed. Use alternative field at Benghazi.' With that the control tower radio went dead.

Ritter's eyes flew to the petrol gauge. They were low on fuel. They couldn't possibly make it to the other field. But the ashen-faced agent team had no time to consider that possibility. '*Enemy bombers,*' the rear gunner yelled over the intercom. The pilot reacted at once. He threw the Heinkel into a wild, diving curve. They escaped into the cloud cover, but their troubles were not over. Suddenly the left engine went dead. The other one started to splutter and cough, as if it might go out at any moment. The Heinkel began to shake violently. They would have to make a forced landing. But where? The pilot clicked on the plane's searchlight. To their horror they saw that they were over the sea.

As the major remembered after the war, 'We saw nothing but the deep blue of midnight African sky. All we could hear was the howl of the wind over the wings. Suddenly there was a blow as hard as steel. That was the last thing that my mind registered.'

Ritter's career in the *Abwehr* was over.

4

While Ritter was recovering from the crash in hospital Canaris took charge of the next Condor expedition which successfully infiltrated Brandenburgers into the heart of the enemy camp in Cairo. At the same time he was actively considering other operations which would hurt the British Empire. He had come to the conclusion that the world's two major canals, Suez and Panama, were the most vulnerable bottlenecks through which most of the Empire's supplies came. If he could knock them out, Britain might well be finished. The next Condor op might deal with Suez. But what about the Panama Canal, four thousand miles away on the other side of the Atlantic?

For a while he toyed with a plan to destroy all the key locks along the length of the canal. Two U-boats would take two Stuka dive-bombers, broken up and in crates, to some secluded bay off the South American coast. Here specially trained *Luftwaffe* ground crews would reassemble the planes within forty-eight hours, as they had been trained to do. Thereupon, as soon as the U-boats had departed, the two pilots would carry out their mission. Naturally they would have to abandon their planes in the end, but it was hoped that they would be able to reach the pro-German haven of Argentina by that time. In due course, they would be repatriated to the Reich. But before the plan could be carried out and the U-boats were ready to sail from the French port of Lorient the expedition was betrayed and had to be cancelled.

By now the Admiral had hatched another plot. The main sources of paying for the Eighth Army's supplies were the gold and diamond mines of South Africa. How was he going to sabotage the transport of the gold and the diamonds to London where they were sold to raise the foreign currency that Britain needed to buy supplies overseas? How were they taken to the UK? Where were they assembled in South Africa for dispatch?

If we are to believe sources close to the Brandenburgers, Canaris found a South African renegade who had a twin brother working in the London bureau of the capital's leading diamond merchant in Hatton Garden. This brother was put out of action one morning by his twin. Clad in his brother's bowler, carrying his furled umbrella and a copy of *The Times*, the renegade entered the Hatton Garden offices and found out the sailing dates of the Royal Navy's submarines bringing the diamonds to Britain.

With this information, Canaris set about planning a bold action which, he thought originally, might need the whole Brandenburg Regiment to carry out. On 1 April, 1941, a commandeered French yacht set sail from France bound for Africa. It was skippered by an old Hamburg seadog, Captain Hansen. The yacht carried three Brandenburgers, the brother of the diamond merchant in London, a radio operator named Fritz Braun, who had spent many years in South Africa as a travelling salesman, and a fanatical anti-British Boer. Tom Moore (probably a faked name) had been a member of the pro-Nazi South African *Broederbond*, which the Brandenburgers hoped to enlist in their attempts to sabotage the bullion shipments.

On Sunday, 9 June they arrived off the Green River, some 150 nautical miles from Cape Town. Here the three Brandenburgers risked the six-foot high surf to land safely in Boer territory. Now they split up, with Moore and his radio operator seeking refuge with friendly Boer families on the Veldt.

Within the month the Brandenburgers and their Boer helpers,

with long memories of British oppression, started sabotaging government installations, railway lines and bridges – all vital for the carriage of the diamonds and gold to the ports. As reports of their successes began to filter back to Canaris in Berlin, he decided to send four more Brandenburgers to join them. This time they would travel by U-boat. But the landing was not successful. When the U-boat surfaced it was spotted by a British destroyer. The captain yelled, 'Alarm stations,' with two of the Brandenburgers in their rubber dinghy and two about to mount the conning tower to join them. The U-boat's tanks started to flood and it began to submerge. Too late! The destroyer surged forward, a white bone in her teeth. Depth charges exploded all around her, sending her rocking wildly from side to side,while the two agents in the dinghy grabbed madly for the stanchion on the conning tower and were about to be dragged under. But they were in luck. A third depth charge forced the U-boat to the surface. The Brandenburgers were hauled up the nets by the jubilant British sailors, to be followed minutes later by the U-boat survivors, drenched in oil and choking from the sea water they had swallowed.

The Brandenburgers had, however, been trained what to say if they were captured. They told their interrogators that they were just two other members of the U-boat's crew. It didn't seem to puzzle their interrogators that they were dressed in rough civilian clothes. Nor did they ask what the two had been doing in the rubber boat. As a result they were sent after a while to a normal German POW camp where to their surprise they were contacted almost immediately by Moore's radioman, Fritz Braun. He had bad news. Both he and Moore had been captured by the South African Police during a sabotage operation. Braun didn't know where the police were keeping Moore, they kept switching him from camp to camp every month, as if the Police realized that he was the ringleader of the Boer saboteurs and were afraid his comrades would try to rescue him.

Braun, who had told his captors that he was an ordinary German merchant seaman forced to help Moore, waited till he was contacted from the outside. He was, within forty-eight hours. Together he and the other two Brandenburgers, Lutz and Friedrich, were smuggled out of the POW camp, probably with the connivance of the guards, many of whom were Boer sympathizers.

35

Their rescuer, a German-South African named von Sangen, said that Tom Moore was being held in the naval prison at St John. The three then decided that they'd get Moore out somehow or other, because they would need him in the new plan with which Lutz and Friedrich had been sent from Berlin.

Together with their new-found Boer friends, they chartered a small ship and sailed to St John. Dressed in British uniforms and with well-forged papers, they managed to convince the British commandant of the prison that they had orders to take Moore to the provincial capital. Within an hour of his release Moore had changed into civilian clothes at a neighbouring Boer farm and was on his way with the rest to Kimberley, the centre of the diamond industry, some three hundred miles away.

On their way they revealed the new plan that Canaris had given them. It was to stop the supply of diamonds at source. If they could do that it would put British supply purchases in the Argentine, the USA and elsewhere back for months. The supply of pounds to buy these essential war goods was running out rapidly. London vitally needed the diamonds to exchange for foreign currency.

Unfortunately Moore had lost his nerve in prison and he refused to go along with the plan. Many of their Boer helpers also backed out. Everywhere in the Rand there were supplies of high explosives, but the Boers refused to help them to obtain any. So they went it alone.

They had already discovered where the diamonds for the next London shipment were stored and that they had only three days in which to destroy them. Time was running out. Braun now drove to Pretoria where he managed to buy the necessary high explosives. In their hotel room they constructed primitive and dangerous detonators which they tried out in the wastes around Kimberley at night. Now they were ready. If they succeeded, London would lose several months' production of the vital diamonds.

The night was hot and still. As Lutz reported later, the only noise was the drunken singing of the mine-workers, who drank thin beer by the gallon to drown their sorrows and forget till the morrow their terrible existence underground. Carefully Friedrich parked the borrowed car and started unpacking their gear at the back entrance to the storage building. There wasn't a guard to be seen in a place that was usually full of guards (the diamond mine workers were searched rigorously after every shift). Industrial diamonds were of no interest to the ordinary thief and who would suspect that thousands of miles from the fighting front German agents would soon be going into action? Just like the Africans, the white guards were probably also enjoying their evening beer.

Lutz whispered, 'Everything's okay. The guards have just finished their routine inspection.'

Now they went into action. Lutz and Braun cut through the wire which encircled the building and helped Friedrich to carry the high explosive through. Crouched in their cover – a few parched dusty bushes – Lutz pointed to a row of windows on the ground floor. They were just visible in the dim light of the nearest street lamp (there was no black-out in South Africa). 'The second window leads to the heating system. We're going in there.'

They sped forward, crouched low. No one spotted the three silent shadows as they hurried across the empty yard. A couple of tugs and Lutz had the window open. One after another they dropped into the warmth of the cellar. Lutz clicked on his flashlight. In its harsh light they could see the whitewashed walls and boilers.

'On the other side of that wall,' Lutz whispered, 'is the chamber which contains the diamonds. If we blow through it, we've got them'.

The others knew it wouldn't be that easy. They had been unable to measure the full impact of their explosives in the rough tests they had carried out in the veldt outside Kimberley. Too much explosive and they wouldn't live to tell the tale. Too little and nothing would happen.

Now Braun was told to find the fusebox. 'As soon as the explosive is fired,' Friedrich ordered the radioman, 'we've got to be ready to break the circuits and stop the alarm system. All right?' Braun nodded his understanding.

Friedrich placed the explosives and payed out the cable. Then the three of them took up their positions behind the steel door of the boiler room.

'Now!' Friedrich snapped. Braun hurried to the fuse box and cut the connection. A hiss was followed by a dull red spark running the length of the cable. The next moment there was a dull explosion. Automatically the Brandenburgers opened their mouths to prevent their eardrums from bursting. Acrid smoke flooded the cellar, making them cough and splutter. But the explosive had worked. When the smoke cleared they saw that they had blown a hole in the wall large enough for them to get through. Hastily they went to work. Although they had cut the alarm system which would have brought reinforcements from the nearest police station – and police stations were everywhere in the diamond district – the police might have heard the muffled explosion and be on their way already.

After they had crawled through the hole they placed three new charges around the huge safe which contained the diamonds. Each man placed his own charge and covered it with bricks and mortar from the shattered wall. Then they backed off, took cover behind the steel door and detonated the charges. The wall around the safe crumbled. The great steel safe sagged at a crazy angle.

The men needed no second invitation. They picked up the big leather sacks they had brought with them and started to cram them full of the sparkling loot. Sweat poured down their foreheads as they worked, alert for the first angry shouts which would mean they had been discovered.

But they were lucky. Five minutes later they had completed the looting of the Oppenheimer Diamond Company's safe and were running to their waiting car, driven by one of their pro-Nazi Boer assistants.

They drove at high speed in the direction of Bloemfontein. But Friedrich had no eyes for the night scenery, spectacular as it was. He was bent over his map, following their progress in anxious detail. Finally he told the South African driver, 'All right, you can stop in two hundred metres.'

With amazing precision he had found the spot that he and Lutz had worked out with their chief months before – a small sideroad, leading off to the rolling plain, covered by high parched grass.

There they left their South African accomplice. Before he went, the Boer said, 'Let's hope we can meet again in Kimberley in better times after the war.' The three Germans expressed the same sentiment. But there would be no reunion in Africa for the Brandenburgers after the bitter defeat of 1945. Only one of them would survive the war and live to tell his tale of high adventure.

Some time later they cleared a rough-and-ready landing strip. Then they lit a grass fire at each end of it and waited, moving only to keep the smoke rising, watching the dawn sky anxiously.

It seemed an age before the great four-engined plane appeared in the sky. It had flown from its base in Southern France in answer to their call on their long-range portable *Abwehr* transmitter. They had been rescued.

The longest and perhaps boldest of all the Brandenburgers' operations in the Second World War had ended in one hundred per cent success. Working on plans conceived in Berlin by staff officers who had probably never even seen Kimberley, the three amateur safe-crackers had got away with several million pounds' worth of diamonds and had levelled a significant blow at Britain's war economy. It was quite an achievement.

It was not surprising, therefore, that they felt they had well earned the gift which was now presented to them by the Condor's second pilot, who said, 'Admiral Canaris said he wanted you to drink it on the flight home if you pulled the job off.'

It was a double magnum of the best French champagne bought with the white-haired spymaster's own money.

Three: Operation Condor
1942

'In the next few weeks I need an absolutely reliable unit in Egypt. It is absolutely essential for the success of my planned offensive.'

Rommel to Admiral Canaris, 1942.

On 14 May, 1942, the newly appointed Protector of Bohemia and Moravia, i.e. Czechoslovakia, received his former superior officer in the feudal splendour of his castle in occupied Prague.

Since Heydrich and Canaris had last met, the former had worked his way high up the ladder. Although the Führer had forbidden him to do so – he knew too many secrets – he had flown sorties into Russia, had been shot down way behind the enemy front and had successfully made his way back. His chest was now covered with the medals he had won during these secret forays.

In September, 1941, he had been appointed to take over occupied Czechoslovakia and make it work for the German war machine. He had jumped at the chance. As he had told his wife at the time, 'Up to now my career has been negative. Now I'm going to do something positive. I'm sick of getting rid of people, putting them behind bars. This is my chance to do something with a purpose.'

Heydrich had soon exterminated the Czech intelligentsia, the backbone of the country's resistance to their German occupiers. At the same time he had spoiled the workers, who were vital to the German war machine, giving them better rations, long holidays at the government's expense, improved working conditions and had introduced the first health insurance scheme in the republic's short existence.

But there was one small fly in the ointment which annoyed Heydrich. There was a major spy loose in Prague who was signalling to London. This Heydrich knew because his radio detector vans were picking up his signals. But time and again the agent, known by his cover name of 'A54', escaped the vans.

43

The knowledge that the unknown agent was evading his best Gestapo men infuriated Heydrich, so he formed a special squad, designated 'Traitor X Group', consisting of Gestapo men, police officials and SS men, to catch him.

In the end this special squad arrested the super spy who, as they would learn later after interrogation and torture, had been working in their midst for years. Not only was he not a Czech, but a *German* and a first name friend of no less a person than Heydrich's boss himself, Himmler! *He was also a key member of the* Abwehr *in Czechoslovakia!*

At first Heydrich had been furious at the discovery and had been all for having him executed on the spot. Later, however, when he had arranged that Paul Thuemmel, as the agent was named, was kicked out of the Nazi Party and all traces of his long-term relationship with Himmler were removed, Heydrich realized that he could used Thuemmel's membership of the *Abwehr* as a weapon against Canaris. Thuemmel would help him to dig the grave of the hated military espionage service, after which the SS would take over the whole business of spying and sabotage.

This is why he had called the conference that day in May. As Heydrich and Canaris entered, the latter noted that his most deadly enemy, 'Gestapo' Mueller, the head of the secret police, was present. That was a bad sign.

Heydrich rose to speak first. He had several bones to pick with Canaris. He disliked the fact that Canaris employed many Jews in his spy organization – indeed two of his best agents spying on Soviet Russia were Jews. He also disliked the fact that Canaris had used Russian nationals in his Brandenburg Regiment. In particular it had angered him that 'Battalion Nightingale' (*Nachtigall*), under the command of Captain Harzner who had fired the first shots of the war, contained three companies of Ukrainians, who had raised the flag of Ukrainian independence when they had marched into Russia the previous June. Promptly Heydrich's liquidation squads, sent to that country to wipe out nationalists, Jews and the like, had arrested the Ukrainian nationalist leader, Stefen Bandera. In short, Heydrich was determined to have it out with his former superior and take over control of his organization.

However his speech was relatively mild. He was leaving it to his subordinates to mount the attack. He finished his address and nodded to Canaris. The latter knew what was expected of him at this moment of crisis between the two services. He put forward a string of positive suggestions for better co-operation. But, despite his eloquence, the faces of the assembled Gestapo and SD officers remained stony.

The reason was clear when Mueller, a shaven-headed Bavarian with a face which looked as if it had been carved out of granite, rose to speak. Mueller made no attempt to conceal his contempt for Canaris and his organization. For years now he had been after the group of anti-Hitlerites around Oster, but with no success. Even though he knew that someone, but he didn't know who, was protecting Oster and the other traitors in the *Abwehr* HQ in Berlin, he felt sufficiently strong to attack Canaris and his 'old-fashioned bureaucratic organization' all along the line. How else could traitors like Paul Thuemmel have managed to get away with it for so long?

Canaris's sallow face flushed a little, but his hooded eyes revealed nothing. He knew Mueller was nothing without Heydrich and, although the latter was a very powerful man indeed, he, too, was having his troubles. Among other things, he had incurred the displeasure of the second most powerful man in the Nazi Party, Hitler's *eminence grise*, Martin Bormann.

All the same Canaris was shocked when Heydrich started to sum up the results of the days' conference. Looking directly at Canaris, he said, 'Because of the situation at home and abroad, the organization and personnel of the *Abwehr* must be changed. The present officers of the *Abwehr* have shown that they are incapable and they must be replaced by new men from the SS. In the interest of the Reich's security, there must be a centralized Secret Service organization. Its representatives must have the power to act in all departments and to draw on the total manpower. These men would be responsible to their ministers, the Minister of State *and to me*.'

Heydrich looked hard at Canaris as he said those last words. He knew from his spies that Canaris was falling apart. Nowadays the Admiral often appeared in his office with his uniform buttoned the wrong way and with food stains and cigar ash on his tunic. Once, in Spain, he had stood up in the back seat of his open car and saluted a flock of sheep, declaring, 'You never know, one of my superiors might be hidden among them.' He spent hours meditating in the gloom of Catholic churches. Once he had suggested to one of his subordinates in Greece, whom he had asked what he was going to do after the war, 'Why we'll open a *taverna*. I'll make the coffee and you can serve the food.' In other words, Heydrich thought that Canaris was on the skids.

But indirectly Paul Thuemmel, his one-time agent, saved Canaris – for a while. Agent 'A54' had kept London well informed of the new state of the Czech working class which was actively co-operating with the German occupiers. War production was mounting. Skoda factories were turning out tanks and guns for the Germans by the hundred. Something had to be done by the Allies to stop the Czechs from collaborating.

The result was that Heydrich was assassinated by Czech parachutists flown from Britain. The expected German reprisals, including the notorious Lidice massacre, alienated the Czech workers from their new German masters and industrial production fell.

2

A month earlier, Canaris, always on the move, had been in North Africa with Rommel. He turned up in grey flannels and a poor quality black jacket he had picked up in a Spanish flea market. Rommel, on the other hand, made no concessions to the desert heat. He didn't wear the yellow uniform of his *Afrika Korps*. Instead he wore the thick field grey of the regular army. But round his bull-like neck he had wound a brightly coloured scarf and on his cap he wore a pair of captured British goggles.

Quickly and confidently Rommel briefed Canaris's Brandenburgers and the two agents who were to go to Cairo on his new offensive, which he believed would take him to Cairo. He ended by saying 'Before us we are faced with a major task: to drive to the Suez Canal and take Egypt. If we succeed – and we *must* succeed – then the British will lose the whole of the Near East.'

He turned to the men of the Brandenburg Regiment who were to make up the infiltration team, in particular to 'Sandy' and 'Buddy', as they now called themselves, and who would be the first to go. 'We need information about the enemy's intentions,' he said. 'Fullers* might change his code. By that time I need

* Ironically enough Rommel's primary source of information in Cairo was the

another network built up in Cairo. For that reason,' he said, 'I have taken up your suggestion to run a new team in before our old network folds up. In the next few weeks I want an absolutely reliable unit in Egypt. It is essential for the success of my planned offensive. I don't want a second failure like that business of the aeroplane,' referring to the abortive Ritter mission.

To this Canaris replied, 'I am afraid that we can never give a hundred per cent assurance that things will work out well, but this time I am inclined to think that everything will be all right.' He nodded to 'Buddy', a small, thick-set Brandenburger who wore a captain's uniform. 'Captain Eppler and I selected the group personally. They've all spent years in the Orient, speak English perfectly and in some cases Arabic. The doctors have inspected them and they are absolutely fit to face up to the rigours of the desert.'

Rommel then relaxed somewhat. Turning to Count Almaszy, who was going to guide the Brandenburgers through the trackless desert, he said, 'It's a bold plan. I hope you don't die in the damned desert.'

The Hungarian smiled. 'If you knew how many times I've been through that damned desert, *Herr Generalfeldmarschall*, then you'd believe we can do it.'

Rommel shrugged. 'Oh well, lunatics are usually lucky. Why shouldn't you be?' And with that he went, leaving the Brandenburgers to discuss the details of the operation with Admiral Canaris. Now everything depended upon an elderly Hungarian and the strange-looking Captain Eppler, alias 'Buddy'.

Johannes Eppler had been born in Alexandria, the son of German parents. His father had died when he was six months old and two years later his mother married a wealthy Egyptian, Gafer Pasha, who brought up his adopted son as a Muslim and by the time Eppler left school he could speak fluent English, German and Arabic.

But he had not turned out as his serious, well-connected father had hoped. He spent much of his time in Cairo's night clubs, at the racecourse or with ladies of easy virtue. As the future President of Egypt, Sadat, wrote of Eppler in his *The Secret*

US military attaché, Lieutenant-Colonel Fullers, who was allowed access to virtually all the British Eighth Army's secrets. His signals code had been broken by the *Abwehr*. Rommel gained most of his intelligence from this source.

Diary of the Revolution, 'The boy had not matched up to the hopes placed in him. Under the influence of doubtful companions, he spent his nights in suspicious establishments, much to the sorrow of his father who finally gave up on him.'

In 1939, however, when war broke out, Eppler remembered his German blood. He returned to the Reich and volunteered for the tank corps. But his superiors soon saw that there was more to Eppler than a future tank gunner. With his background and knowledge of languages he would be better off in intelligence.

He was summoned to the Berlin HQ of the *Abwehr*, where he was interviewed, 'I shall never forget the name of the man who recruited me,' Eppler recalled years later. 'He was called Major Boehne. He put me through my paces and then accepted me into the organization from which I was freed years later with a broken nose and a crushed kidney.'

Two years of training had followed at the Brandenburgers' training camps in Düren and Brandenburg. Now he was returning to Cairo to be used in an operation about which he had long dreamed.

With Almaszy as guide, the two-truck Brandenburg expedition would leave the coastal road and enter the desert just beyond the last Italian outpost at Jalo Oasis. Driving due south the Brandenburgers would head for the Kufra Oasis. Here they would turn east to cross the Libyan-Egyptian border.

Almaszy would guide them through the Japsa Pass in the Glif Kebir Plateau, a pass which the Hungarian had reconnoitred in 1937. 'One of nature's airfields,' as he told Eppler. 'When I saw it for the first time in 1937 I was struck by it then. Now I realize one could land squadron after squadron right there behind the British line.'

There Almaszy would survey the area – still a blank on the map in 1942 – for Rommel before proceeding through the first British-held oasis, El Kharga. Once that obstacle had been overcome, Eppler and Sandy, whose real name was Sandberg, would make their way alone to the railhead where they would board a train for Cairo. Here Sandy would assume the role of an American civilian, named Peter Monkcaster, while Eppler would slip back into his old role as Hussein Gafar.

It was a bold but dangerous plan. The ten-man-strong Brandenburg team were all young and fit, but none of them realized what desert travel over hundreds of miles really meant. Then there was the problem of whether Eppler and Sandberg could be relied upon once they reached Cairo. For they carried with them a bag stuffed with English five pound notes, some twenty thousand pounds in all, a fortune in those days. Would they not simply desert with the money, forgetting their dangerous mission in favour of the capital's fleshpots?

In Berlin one of Canaris's staff officers had pointed this risk out to his chief, but Canaris had waved him away, telling the suspicious officer that he had full confidence in his two playboy agents.

Now the preparations were complete. After some last discussion about the code Sandy would use to send his messages to Rommel's HQ (it would be based on Daphne du Maurier's novel *Rebecca*), Canaris stretched out his hand to Eppler and then the others, repeating the same tired phrases which old men so often use to send young men to their death, 'I'd like to wish you the best of luck,' to each one in turn.

3

The expedition, two trucks and three jeeps, got off to a good start. The weather was excellent and visibility so good that they could see up to fifty kilometres. They rolled by Roman ruins and newer ones caused by the battles which had swayed back and forth across this stretch of coastal road for the last two years.

After two hours or so they turned off the Via Balbia and set out into the desert. For kilometre after kilometre they followed a rough sand road, heading for Jalo Oasis, which they left the following day and hit the desert proper.

As Eppler wrote of that first encounter with the desert much later, 'it is merciless. It destroys everyone who goes into it without training. Fanaticism and fatalism are the products of the desert.' But his men were trained and they wouldn't succumb to fatalism. There was too much to do every time the vehicles got stuck. As yet the going was comparatively good – flat hard sand that stretched to the burning horizon. Their only real problem at this time was navigation. The Italian maps they were using were no good, but Almaszy seemed to be finding his way all right, even without the maps.

Another day passed. They saw a plane, a tiny black speck in

the hard blue sky. But they were in a part of the desert where no one had ever been before and they reasoned that the pilot probably never even looked down.

Then the sand started to cause them problems, especially the dunes. Almaszy gathered the five drivers together and told them how to take the dunes, some of which were as high as a house: 'Position your vehicle directly facing the top of the dune,' he explained. 'Then let her have it. Drive at top speed for the crest. Once on top brake hard momentarily, swing to left or right and go down at an angle. If you don't, you'll go down – *straight* down – twenty or thirty metres. Then the doctor here won't be much use to you.' He pointed to the red-faced *Unterarzt*, who seemed to be suffering from the heat most of all.

They struggled on. Time and again one of the vehicles got bogged down in the sand and they had to go through the back-breaking process of unloading everything, digging trenches beneath the wheels and slipping metal strips into them so that the wheels could gain some purchase. Sometimes they did it twenty times a day.

The strain started to tell and they began to suffer casualties. Their chief technician, a staff sergeant, collapsed with an apparent heart attack. Apparent because the little doctor had gone temporarily crazy and they had been forced to knock him out and tie him up in the back of one of the trucks,

They tried to go on, but with two casualties, Almaszy knew they couldn't do it. They needed the full complement of ten men. So, after being out in the uncharted desert for four days, the little expedition was forced to turn round and go back to the Italian fort at Jalo,

On 11 May they tried again. With them they had three new volunteers from the Brandenburger Regiment. They had had it drilled into them that if anyone fell sick and threatened to endanger the mission, he was to take his own life.

Sandy, who was slipping more and more into his role of the hard-bitten Yank, commented half in English, half in German, 'No one will die, don't worry. *Unkraut vergeht nicht* (weeds don't snuff it).' The other Brandenburgers laughed and hoped he was right.

The misery started once again – sun, sand, sweat and a steady persistent thirst in temperatures which had risen to 120 degrees. Almaszy didn't seem to notice the terrible conditions. Whenever he heard anyone complaining he'd say, 'Have you never stopped to think that somewhere at this moment other people are not simply having to exist in this heat? *They are having to fight in it!*' That usually stopped the complaints for a while, but only for a while.

Four days later they spotted some vehicles. They had just cleared yet another sand dune when one of the sergeants cried, 'Trucks to the north!' Almaszy had already told him they mustn't think they were alone in this unexplored desert. There were Englishmen out here too – members of the famed Long Range Desert Group and the newly formed Special Air Service under David Stirling. They also used the trackless waste as a way round the German front.

While the others scattered behind whatever cover they could find, Almaszy and Eppler crept forward and observed a group of black dots in the distance. Staring through their binoculars they made out a circle of trucks formed up like American pioneers might have done with their 'prairie schooners' before an Indian attack.

'They look like the Lawrence patrol,' Almaszy said after a while He meant a Long Range patrol led by Major Clapton, whom Almaszy had known before the war in Cairo. He called his group after T. E. Lawrence of First World War fame. 'He's obviously left them there as a base for one of his patrols.'

The Hungarian explained that whenever the British went out on a lengthy mission they left behind them at certain points vehicles containing food, water and spare parts. Clapton had adopted the idea from the Arabs, who never ventured into the desert without two camels, just in case one died. 'God has sent us those trucks,' Almaszy said, admitting for the first time that he had been worried about their supply position.

After helping themselves to the British supplies, the Branden-burgers pushed on. The men were becoming jumpy, but after six days in the desert the men were about at the end of their tether. One of the young officers had gone mad with heat and was now tied up in the back of a truck. More importantly, their water supply had nearly run out. It was then that Almaszy pointed to the Kebir Mountains shimmering in the far distance. 'Up there we'll find water,' he announced. 'We have only to find a pass. If we do, I'll give you water. When I was here in 1937, I buried a water depot up there.'

Eppler could hardly believe his ears. Water buried five years before! It was impossible. But he said nothing. He didn't want to destroy the remaining faith of his men.

Five hours later they found the pass – and the water. Almaszy stopped the lead truck and asked for a spade. He dropped from the running board and started to dig. Suddenly his blade struck metal. Turning to Eppler, he said, 'What did I tell you? That's genuine filtered water from the Nile. Five years ago I put it here in English cans, just in case.' He cleared away the last of the sand to reveal a layer of two-gallon cans. 'Look, they're still sealed.'

'And you mean you can still drink that stuff after five years?' Eppler asked.

'Drink it! That's not the word for it,' he cried enthusiastically. 'We shall savour it like a gift from the Gods.'

It was on that same day, 18 May, 1942, that, two and a half thousand miles away in Prague, Canaris faced up to Heydrich and his henchmen, knowing that Heydrich was now definitely out to get him.

On 22 May, 1942, after eleven days in the desert, the little team of Brandenburgers saw the first lights in the desert dusk. They were well within Egyptian territory by now and had arrived just outside the El Kharga Oasis, which Almaszy knew was occupied by British troops.

The Count stopped the convoy and announced, 'We have reached our destination.'

Eppler stared down at the twinkling lights in the distance and experienced, as he wrote later, 'a strange feeling. After days out in the desert, down there were people, eating, drinking, smoking – perhaps even making love.'

Almaszy tapped Eppler on the shoulder and said, 'Tomorrow you're on your own. I think tonight Sandy and you should celebrate. I've got a few cans of Canadian food left and a little bit of whisky.'

They passed through the large oasis without any difficulty. Their khaki uniforms and trucks appeared no different from those of the British troops stationed out here in the middle of nowhere. On the other side of the oasis Almaszy and the other Brandenburgers said their farewells and turned round to begin their long journey back to Libya. The two agents waited till they had disappeared, then changed into their civilian clothes. Thereupon they lifted up their heavy cases, which contained their radio and the twenty thousand pounds and headed for the little station which linked this remote outpost with Cairo, the Egyptian capital. The first stage of their long trek was over.

The two agents soon found friends in the happy-go-lucky international set which still inhabited Cairo. They rented a houseboat on the Nile next to one occupied by an English officer reputedly the head of British counter-intelligence in the capital. Now they began to set up a new network that would supply Rommel with the information he needed for his drive on Cairo and the Nile. It wasn't difficult.

Through a dark-haired belly dancer named Hekmath, who had many 'friends' among the staff officers of the British GHQ, they were soon obtaining a great deal of confidential information. At the same time they formed links with the group of young nationalist officers who wanted to throw out the enormously fat and depraved King Farouk, whom they regarded as little better than a British puppet, kept in line by British money, a string of nubile mistresses and his huge collection of pornography.

But their link, a young signals captain in the Egyptian Army named Sadat, was a little suspicious of Eppler, who he thought was little better than an international playboy. As Eppler wrote later, 'As soon as he [Sadat] entered our houseboat and saw the somewhat pompous living room, I could see the look of rejection on his face. He didn't seem to realize that, as the son of a very rich father, I had to live in such circumstances in order to maintain my cover.'

But the Egyptian signals officer, who was to die at the hand of an assassin after becoming President of Egypt, proved a disappointment to the Brandenburgers. 'Sadat was too loud,' Eppler told a newspaper correspondent twenty years later, 'too passionate. He could have betrayed us unwittingly at any moment. I was forced to drop him.'

In the end Eppler broke off all contact with the Egyptian underground. It would be another two decades before it finally achieved its aim. And there was further disappointment in store for him. Through another belly dancer, who performed nightly at the celebrated Kit-Kat Club, he obtained vital information about the Eighth Army's intentions in the Western Desert.

But Sandy, his radio operator, simply could not raise the *Abwehr* listening post in the *Afrika Korps*. Night after night he tried to contact the station with the little radio built into the bar of the houseboat. 'This is Condor,' he would signal. 'This is Condor. Are you receiving me?' But no one ever answered. It seemed as if the *Afrika Korps* had vanished from the desert.

The reason was simple. By a bureaucratic mistake the radio station had been sent to the front and captured in a surprise attack by British infantry. Almost immediately one of the German operators revealed that the *Abwehr* had been intercepting Colonel Fullers' messages to the States all along. Further evidence revealed that there was a second spy ring in Cairo somewhere. Time was running out for Sandy and Buddy.

On 14 October, 1942, the whole plan, one hitherto without parallel in the history of German espionage, came to an abrupt end. Sandy and Buddy were in their houseboat trying to raise the listening station, for now they knew that the new commander in the Western Desert, General Montgomery, was going to make his final stand at El Alamein. He had formulated a make-or-break situation. There would be no more retreats to Cairo. His Eighth Army would fight and die – or win – at that remote little railway station.

Suddenly there was a thunderous knocking on the door, followed by the sound of heavy boots running across the deck above their heads. They had been discovered at last.

'Okay,' Sandy said, still playing cool and tough, 'Look after yourself, Buddy. Goodbye *Hauptmann* Eppler.'

The knocking gave way to the sound of rifle butts knocking down the door. Frantically the two Brandenburgers attempted to destroy their papers. 'You see to the radio!' Eppler yelled in German and rushed to the door in an attempt to delay the intruders.

The door flew open and Captain 'Sammy' Sansom, with whom Eppler had often played golf in the last few months, stood there, pistol in hand. Behind him stood a squad of British MPs, all levelling their stens guns or revolvers.

Slowly Eppler raised his hands. His career as a spy was over. That terrible twelve-day trek over two thousand miles of uncharted desert had been for nothing.

On 23 October General Montgomery surprised Rommel at El Alamein. It was a hard-fought battle that lasted nearly two weeks. But in the end the commander of the Eighth Army won. German power in the Dark Continent was almost finished. Six months later they were run out of Africa for good.

Oberleutnant Heinz Schmidt had once been Rommel's aide. Now he had returned to his old unit, Special Group 288, which had originally been trained for special duties in Iran in 1941 when it had been planned to use the Brandenburgers to aid a local revolt against the British. Nothing had come of it. Now the unit was fighting against the Americans in North Africa. The day before St Valentine's Day, 1943, Rommel, sick of being forced to retreat by Montgomery, had lashed out at the Americans. He wanted to take one last victim with him before he died. In the Kasserine area he had caught the *Amis*, as he called them contemptuously, off guard. Parts of two US divisions, the 1st Infantry 'The Big Red One', and the 1st Armored, had been forced back. Now Rommel intended to put the whole of US General Fredendall's Second Corps to flight. By this means he hoped that Montgomery's advance might be stopped for a while at least. It was to be *Hauptmann* Schmidt's job to ensure that the *Amis* didn't recover and dig in.

Now Schmidt and his men, with the handful of US prisoners they had already taken, hid in a wadi, listening to the noises of the *Amis* to their immediate front. Suddenly tracer zipped through the darkness. Schmidt had forgotten to warn the machine gunner up the road not to open fire and reveal their position.

The Americans reacted promptly. Five Shermans rumbled forward. When they saw the Germans crouching in the rocks on both sides of the pass, their drivers panicked. They swung the tanks round in a flurry of dust and scuttled to the rear.

Relative silence returned to the battlefield to come. Here and there a machine gun chattered. Occasionally signal flares sailed into the sky. But the guns had stopped and the *Amis* had ceased making any noise to their front. Schmidt hesitated. What if he was walking into a trap? Were the American infantrymen waiting for him to stumble into their prepared position?

In the end he knew he couldn't wait any longer. Soon he'd have Rommel himself breathing down his neck, for at dawn he was coming to inspect the battlefield personally; and Schmidt knew all about Rommel's temper. He started forward with his group. The real Battle of the Kasserine Pass had begun.

The Brandenburgers' role at Kasserine was not one of great

importance, but it was their first battle fought against the Americans. It was also to be the start of their involvement in more conventional actions.

For now the outfit, soon to be 'Division Brandenburg', was slipping out of the control of Admiral Canaris and into that of Colonel-General Albert Jodl, Hitler's military adviser. The result would be that, later in the year, the Brandenburgers would no longer be engaged in covert operations. Instead they would fight increasingly as conventional infantry, suffering the high losses of formations that stayed in the line, especially in Russia, until they were bled white. The battle of the Kasserine Pass in North Africa in February, 1942, marked the passing of an era.

It was dawn and Schmidt had advanced into the pass proper. To his right German engineers were clearing mines with their bayonets. He dismissed the engineers and focused his glasses on the duty road that ran through the pass. An enemy Sherman flying a white flag was rumbling cautiously down it. After a few moments he decided that it didn't want to surrender. It was merely using the white flag to collect the *Ami* casualties of the previous day.

Once the engineers had cleared the mines, Germany's new secret weapon would come rumbling up. It and 'the flying artillery', the Stukas, would soon send the *Amis* running. Then the way through the pass would be clear for Rommel's 10th Panzer Division.

One hour later Germany's new artillery weapons were in position: mobile six-barrelled, electrically-fired artillery pieces, which could launch six 105mm rocket shells and be on the move again within the minute. With a banshee-like howl, the first '*Nebelwerfer*', or 'Moaning Minnie' as it became known to Allied troops, fired its rockets. They raced into the sky, tailing thick black smoke behind them, as the Stukas hurtled out of the heavens. Schmidt jerked his fist up and down three times, the infantry signal for advance, and moved forward with his special troops. That night the Kasserine Pass would be in German hands.

'What happened during the night of 19–20 February,' states the official US history of the campaign in North Africa, 'cannot be clearly reconstructed from the record.'

It is not surprising. Key American units broke and fled, abandoning guns, trucks, jeeps, even tanks. The British Lothian and Border Horse were rushed up to try to plug the gap and were virtually massacred.

Schmidt and his troopers, at the front, did their best to panic the *Amis* even more. They screamed and shouted and bellowed orders in German as if they were a whole battalion. They cried in English, '*All right, you guys, put down your weapons, we're surrendering!*' or '*Bug out ... Everybody's bugging out ... Let's go ... bug out!*'

And indeed it seemed that everybody was 'bugging out'. As dawn approached, two Shermans came rumbling up and spotted Schmidt's advance force. They turned tail immediately, but both got stuck in a wadi. As Schmidt's men raced up to deal with them, 'their crews abandoned them and fled to the rear'.

It was like that everywhere as Rommel's 10th Panzer advanced through the Pass behind Schmidt and his troopers. Two US regimental command posts were overrun. American engineers fled. French gunners, supporting the Americans, abandoned their cannons. All traffic, it seemed, was westwards. Mixed elements of the 1st US Infantry and 1st US Armored Divisions were cut off at the north-western entrance to the Pass. The drivers of the armoured infantry down in the wadi took off, leaving the foot-sloggers to fend for themselves.

In the end, before the situation was stabilized by reinforcements rushed up from both the British and American armies in North Africa, Fredendall's II Corps had lost 6,000 men in dead, wounded and captured, Fredendall was 'kicked upstairs', given a training command in the States, and replaced by the up-and-coming General 'Blood and Guts' Patton.

Schmidt and his troopers, who had helped to start the panic that night in the Kasserine Pass, had done their job well. But never again would they see 'hundreds, perhaps thousands of *Ami* soldiers streaming back to the rear, abandoning their vehicles everywhere'.

But Rommel, sick and angry, was unable to turn the Kasserine victory, America's first defeat in the West in the Second World War, into a much larger one. Feeling let down by the apparent lack of drive of the 10th Panzer Division, he ordered it to withdraw a few days later.

Moodily he watched it pull back. In two weeks from now he would return to the Reich. In just over a year he would be killed, not by the enemy, but by his own hand at Hitler's orders, in retaliation for the help he had given to the plotters who had attempted to kill the Führer, the same group that dated back to the 'Oster Circle' of 1938.

Curiously, on that day of defeat, the officer who would trigger off the chain of circumstances which would mean the end not only of Rommel but also of Admiral Canaris was standing a mere hundred yards away. The Chief of Operations of the 10th Panzer Division was Colonel Klaus von Stauffenberg.

Four: The Most Dangerous Man in Europe
1943

---

*'Why do I have a secret service when they
make such completely unqualified mistakes?'*

Hitler to Canaris, 1943.

In the autumn of 1942 a fat, sleek-haired Munich businessman named Schmidthuber was arrested for smuggling foreign currency out of Germany into neighbouring Switzerland. In that year, by which time many Germans had decided that Hitler had already lost the war, it was a serious but not uncommon breach of Germany's strict currency laws. Schmidthuber, however, was not just another wealthy businessman trying to rescue what he could before the final storm. He was one of Canaris's key agents and the money had been intended for a group of Jewish refugees from Germany who he and others had smuggled out of the country with Canaris's approval.

When Mueller, head of the Secret Police, heard of the arrest, he was very pleased that he finally had something on Canaris whom he hated with a passion. He had been after Canaris and his anti-Hitler plotters in the *Abwehr* for years. Now he sat back and waited to see what Canaris would do. He did nothing.

Schmidthuber, well aware of his fellow Municher's taste for brutal methods, decided to 'sing'. He had a lot to sing about. During his years with the *Abwehr*, he had kept his eyes and ears open. He knew more than Canaris suspected when the latter decided that he wouldn't risk trying to help his employee.

Schmidthuber told his Gestapo interrogators that Colonel Oster had sent a member of the *Abwehr* to the Vatican in 1940 to warn the Holy See, and, naturally, the Belgian Ambassador, that Holland and Belgium were going to be invaded. This confirmed what Mueller had always believed. The traitors who had tipped off the Dutch and the Belgians were inside the *Abwehr*. Schmidthuber also told the Gestapo that a protestant

61

clergyman, Dr Dietrich Bonhoeffer, had been given a passport by the *Abwehr* in order to meet Dr Bell, the British Bishop of Chichester, in Stockholm where they had presumably discussed peace terms. He also confessed that he had smuggled many wealthy Jews, as well as huge sums of money, out of Germany into Switzerland at the behest of the *Abwehr*. All that winter Schmidthuber 'sang', while Germany lost the battles of El Alamein and Stalingrad and the turning point of the war in the Allies' favour was reached.

By April, 1943, Gestapo Mueller and his new associate, General Schellenberg, the up-and-coming head of the *Sichersheitsdienst* (the SS's own spy service), felt they had enough evidence against the *Abwehr* to launch a full-scale investigation into Canaris's service.

On 5 April, 1943, a keen-faced *Luftwaffe* officer, Manfred Roeder, known behind his back as 'the ferret', appeared at the *Abwehr* offices in Tirpitzufer, accompanied by a Gestapo officer, Franz Sonderegger. He asked to see Canaris and was received 'in a very gentlemanly fashion'.

Roeder was not a man for polite chit-chat. He produced his search warrant and asked Canaris to accompany him to the office of one of the Admiral's key officials, Klaus von Dohnanyi, who had long belonged to the group of plotters around the, now, General Oster. Canaris, as polite as ever, rose and accompanied Roeder, leading him through Oster's office – the latter joined them – into von Dohnanyi's room.

Dohnanyi was caught by surprise. Careless as most *Abwehr* officials were, he had at that moment a file on his desk containing details of the meeting with Dr Bell and various other secret activities of the *Abwehr*. Roeder said, 'Please stand away from your desk. I want to search it.'

While Canaris stood in the doorway and Oster stood inside the office itself, Roeder put the incriminating file on another table and began to search the desk. Von Dohnanyi flashed Oster a significant look. Oster caught the direction of his gaze. It was at the damning file, which would mean the end for both of them if Roeder got his hands on it.

Very slowly he moved backwards, his hands behind his back. His fingers touched the file and he started to slip it under his jacket.

Suddenly he was startled by a harsh order, 'Stand still!' It was Sonderegger. All of them looked round, shocked. Even a Gestapo man didn't talk to a German general in that manner. Roeder said calmly, 'General Oster, I request you to hand over to me what you have just taken from that table.'

Oster looked to Canaris for guidance, but the Admiral, whose will to survive was failing, made no sign.

'Hand those papers over to me at once,' Roeder snapped when Oster didn't move.

'What do you mean?' Oster demanded. 'I deny that I have taken anything.'

Roeder turned to Canaris. '*Herr Admiral*,' he said briskly. 'I request you order General Oster to hand over those documents to me.'

'I dont know what documents you mean,' Canaris said. 'I saw nothing.'

'In that case,' Dr Roeder said sharply, 'I shall have to use the powers conferred on me as an examining magistrate.'

Canaris gave in. He nodded to Oster who pulled the papers from his jacket.

Roeder smiled and said to Oster, 'Now leave the room and go to your own office.' He turned to von Dohnanyi. 'Herr von Dohnanyi, open the safe, please.'

'I haven't the key.'

'Then have it fetched at once.'

The key was brought and the safe was opened. It contained plenty of incriminating documents: The records of fifteen Jews sent abroad as 'agents' (all were elderly and one was blind); the details of general staff officers, clergymen, industrialists, who were prepared to co-operate actively in the overthrow of the Nazi regime. It was damning stuff and von Dohnanyi was arrested on the spot while Oster was ordered to place himself at Roeder's disposal in case action was taken against him, too.

Mueller and General Schellenberg of the SD were overjoyed. They had got the 'old fox', as they called Canaris, at last. One of the papers in the safe was marked 'O' in red. For some time they puzzled over the letter which was on top of a list of names of important people. Finally they came to the conclusion that it meant 'organization' and the names were of those who would be prepared to run a post-Hitler Germany. Now they were certain that this meant the end of Admiral Canaris.

But they were in for a great disappointment. Sonderegger was sent to report on the matter to Himmler. He listened to the Gestapo officer's account accepted his written report and the next day returned it to Mueller with the instruction 'Leave the old man alone' written on it in green ink. The whole Schmid-thuber affair had to be dropped immediately. In justification of his decision Himmler said that he was afraid that if the enquiries went any further, 'there is the danger that Canaris might offer to resign his office. This must be avoided at all cost.'

It was a bitter blow to Mueller and even more to Schellenberg, who coveted Canaris' office. But Himmler knew that for the moment Canaris was indispensible. On 10 July, 1943, the Western Allies had landed in Italy. The result had been the fall and abduction of Hitler's fellow dictator, Mussolini. Now the Italo-German alliance was in danger of breaking up. Canaris, with his long experience of Italian affairs and his excellent contacts in that country, was needed more than ever. For a while he had been saved again, but only for a while.

On 29 July Canaris flew to Italy to meet his opposite number, General Amé of the Italian Secret Service. Officially his task was to sound the Italians out. Were they going to stay in the war on Germany's side or not? He was also to try and find out where Mussolini's captors had taken him. Unofficially, he wanted to know how the Italians had managed to get rid of Mussolini with such ease.

During a break in their first meeting, Canaris took Amé by the arm and said, 'Let's get a breath of fresh air.'

Once out of earshot of the others, he said quickly, 'My deepest congratulations on your 25th July (the date of Mussolini's disap-pearance). We need something like that. Germany dreams of being freed from Hitler.'

The astonished Italian decided that he could trust Canaris 'Admiral,' he said, 'I am going to trust you completely. We're trying to gain time. The armistice [with the Allies] will soon be sealed. It's important that Italy is not paralyzed by a sudden Nazi occupation.'

'There's only one way to stop the *Wehrmacht* flooding Italy with new troops,' Canaris replied. 'Try to prevent as many German soldiers coming into your country as possible.'

We do not know General Amé's reaction to those words which

clearly stamped Canaris as a traitor, but we do know that Canaris then said, 'As far as I'm concerned, General Amé, you can rely on me. I won't say anything in Berlin. On the contrary I shall emphasize that Italy is prepared to continue the war on Germany's side. I don't think you can last more than a month. It's vital that you get out of this mess as soon as possible.' With that the two plotters went back to the conference. Two days later he reported to Hitler that Italy would fight on.

One person in particular didn't believe him. That was Schellenberg, who already had his spies in Amé's office. He knew that Amé was part of the group of Italian Army generals and ex-fascist officials who were already dealing with the representatives of the Westen Allies in Lisbon to take Italy out of the war. He knew, too, that Canaris had had a homosexual affair with Amé's chauffeur. Schellenberg used this to blackmail the driver into telling him what was going on in Rome.

He had other sources of information too. In the previous March the Research Institute of the German Post Office had managed to tap the scrambled phone connection used by Churchill in London and Roosevelt in Washington. Now on 29 July, 1943, the Germans heard a very interesting conversation on the Italian situation.

'We don't want proposals for an armistice to be made before we've been definitely approached,' Churchill said. 'That's right,' Roosevelt agreed.

They then talked about the fate of the missing Mussolini. Both agreed that he would 'end up on the hangman's rope'. But how? Churchill was in favour of a show trial which would be 'a healthy lesson for the Nazis'. Roosevelt was against that. Such a trial might affect the coming presidential election. 'Couldn't he just die suddenly?' he suggested, making the point that several of Churchill's enemies had died 'suddenly'* in strange aeroplane accidents.

Roosevelt went on to say, 'I think that if Mussolini died while he was still in Italian hands, we would be best served. . . . If we agree to get rid of him while he is still in their hands . . . there'd be no doubt who had killed him. . . . That wouldn't upset my Italian voters here in the States.'

* These conversations are translated from the German translations of the two statesmen's words.

Churchill wasn't convinced. He said, 'I can't believe that the votes of a handful of Italians in your country can influence your decision.'

Roosevelt didn't pull his punches. 'If I'm not nominated, then I won't be elected. . . . If I lose, our alliance might break up. Stalin will make a separate peace with Germany. Then Hitler will turn his full anger on Britain and, without help, what can you do?'

Churchill still wasn't quite convinced, but there the conversation ended. But when Schellenberg read the transcript he knew all he needed to know. Canaris had lied about Italy's intentions. In addition, Mussolini's life was in real danger. The Duce had to be found and rescued before it was too late!

2

On the late afternoon of 25 July the six officers he had summoned from various parts of Europe stood to attention when Hitler entered the room at his HQ in Rastenburg, East Prussia. Five of them, all field grade officers, saluted rigidly in the Prussian fashion. Surprisingly the sixth bowed from the waist. Hitler looked at him surprise. The SS captain was certainly worth looking at. He was six foot six at least and broad with it. The side of his face was slashed with scars. The dark-haired giant looked a very tough man indeed.

Now one by one the officers stepped forward and introduced themselves until it came to the turn of the big SS man. He took a pace forward and introduced himself: 'Skorzeny, Captain of the SS. Detached from the *Leibstandarte* after service in Russia. Now in charge of the Friedenthal organization.'* Otto Skorzeny had arrived on the scene.

'Which of you know Italy?' Hitler asked.

Skorzeny was the only one who answered. 'I have travelled to Italy twice on a motorbike, as far as Naples, *mein Führer*'

Hitler then asked the assembled officers, 'What do you think of Italy?'

---

* Schellenberger's special SS commando unit, based at the village of Friedenthal, near Berlin, which gave the outfit its name.

66

There was a variety of answers. Some said, 'Loyal ally, member of the anti-comintern pact, our Axis partner.' Hitler looked at Otto Skorzeny. He said simply, 'I am an Austrian, *mein Fuhrer.*' Hitler understood. Skorzeny resented the seizure by the Italians of Austrian territory after the First World War.

Hitler then dismissed the other officers. He had found the man he wanted. 'I have a mission of the highest importance for you,' he announced. 'Mussolini, my friend and our loyal ally, has been arrested by his own people. The Duce represents for me the last great Roman. Under the new government Italy will leave the alliance. But I will maintain my loyalty to my ally. He has to be rescued. Otherwise they will surrender him to the Allies. I order you to find him. This is an all-important mission which will affect the whole course of the war. You must do you utmost to carry out this mission – *and you will succeed.*'

Hitler then went on to tell Skorzeny that he would be placed under the command of General Student who had captured Rotterdam in 1940 and Crete the following year.

'He's already in the picture,' Hitler continued. 'When you leave here you will confer with him and he'll give you further details. But you will be in charge of discovering where Mussolini is. However, the military and diplomatic authorities in Rome are not to learn of your mission. They are completely misinformed about the situation and consequently will react incorrectly.' Hitler paused and fixed Skorzeny with a piercing look. 'Remember,' he went on, 'you are responsible to me personally for the secrecy of this mission. I hope to hear from you soon and wish you all the best.'

Skorzeny clicked his heels. 'I have understood, *mein Führer,*' he said. 'I will do my best.' With that Hitler clasped Skorzeny's hand in both of his. Then Skorzeny saluted, turned about and marched to the door. At the door he turned and faced the dictator once more. Hitler's gaze was fixed upon him 'almost hypnotically' as he said afterwards.

There was little in Skorzeny's early life to explain why he became such a notorious figure during the war and for long afterwards. He was born into a middle-class Viennese business family on 12 June, 1908. After the First World War, in which Austria was defeated and lost her Empire, the Austrian *schilling* was worthless and for a while the Skorzeny children survived on handouts from the International Red Cross. Skorzeny grew up in the worst years of the Depression. For instance he had his first taste of butter at the age of 15, but, as his father said, it was no bad thing to get used to the harshness of life.

In due course he went to the University of Vienna to study engineering and joined one of the traditional German student duelling societies (*die Burschenschaften*). For a century and a half duelling societies had flourished at German-speaking universities where the members drank enormous quantities of beer and fought duels with sabres in order to gain the scars (*die Schmisse*) which would mark them as a university man for the rest of their lives.

Skorzeny fought his first duel in his first year at university and, as he confessed in his memoirs, it was a nerve-wracking experience, 'I could feel my heart beating rapidly. I could only see the face of my opponent very vaguely through the steel grill of my mask. Blade against blade ... with only an occasional pause while the blade of my sabre was disinfected. Then suddenly after the seventh round I felt a short, sharp blow on my head. Surprisingly enough it didn't hurt too much. My only fear was that I had finished. He had not.'

Thereafter Skorzeny fought thirteen more duels which gained him his nickname of 'scarface' among US troops during the Battle of the Bulge. But for him duelling was much more than the means of securing the coveted *Schmisse*: 'I was often grateful later for the self-discipline we learned in our students' club. I never felt as bad under fire as I did at 18 when I had to fight my first duel under the sharp eyes of my fellow students. My knowledge of pain, learned with sabre, taught me not to be afraid of fear. And just as in duelling you must fix your mind on striking at the enemy's head, so, too, in war. You cannot waste time feinting and side-stepping. You must decide on your target and go in.'

Naturally Skorzeny was an ardent Nazi and as soon as the war broke out he volunteered for the *Waffen SS's* elite formation '*Die Leibstandarte Adolf Hitler*' (the Adolf Hitler Bodyguard Regiment). Despite being the oldest volunteer present that day, he was one of only twelve out of scores of volunteers to be accepted. He was posted to the 'Moonlight Company', named for its commander's unpleasant habit of doing most of the company's training at night.

Soon Skorzeny was promoted sergeant and thereafter to the rank of *Fähnrich* (officer-cadet). But as his latter career was to prove he was not cut out to be a conventional soldier. In Holland in 1940 he was drinking in a bar with some comrades when he spotted a portrait of Prince Bernhard, the Prince Consort of Holland, on the wall. German-born Bernhard, now safely lodged in England, had been in the SS himself as a young man. For that reason Skorzeny regarded him as a traitor. He ordered the bar owner to take the portrait down. He refused.

Skorzeny growled, 'If you don't take it down soon, I'll shoot it down.'

But the stubborn Dutchman wouldn't. Skorzeny didn't hesitate. He pulled out his pistol and fired. Drunk as he was, his first shot severed the cord holding up the picture. It fell to the floor shattering the glass. The Dutchman reported the incident to Skorzeny's C.O. The latter, trying to maintain good relations with the Dutch, had Skorzeny's promotion stopped and he was confined to barracks for six weeks.

In 1941 Skorzeny was transferred to the SS Division '*Das Reich*' as an engineer officer in charge of maintaining the division's tanks. Still he saw action enough. Once he was sheltering behind a Russian hut when a salvo of mortar bombs dropped all around them. Skorzeny felt a great blow against the back of his head and blacked out immediately. When he came to a soldier offered him a cigarette. Refusing all medical aid save an aspirin and a glass of schnapps, he went back to his duties. He continued until December of that year when constant headaches and a bad case of stomach colic made it essential that he be evacuated for specialist treatment. That was the end of his conventional military career.

For six months he remained at the depot until one day he was asked to report to the HQ of the *Waffen SS*. There he was told HQ needed 'a technically trained officer' who would be prepared to 'carry out special duties'. That appealed to him. It might mean a break from the boring routine of the depot.

The officer who interviewed him said that the time had come for the SS to set up an unorthodox unit on the lines of the British SAS, one which would operate behind enemy lines. It was a job right up Skorzeny's street.

Thus it was that on 18 April, 1943, Otto Skorzeny became head of the SS's first special troops, four years after the Brandenburgers had been formed. The momentous career of Hitler's 'commando extraordinaire' was about to begin.

Skorzeny had had just time to smoke a badly needed cigarette after his interview with Hitler when an adjutant asked him to come and meet General Student, the head of Germany's Parachute Formations. A moment later he was faced by a bullet-headed *Luftwaffe* general in the blue-green uniform of the paratroops with an ugly red weal on his forehead, the result of a slug fired at him (by his own troops) in Rotterdam two years before.

He told Student about the Führer's instructions. But hardly had he started when the door opened to admit Heinrich Himmler, reputed to be the 'most feared man in Europe'. He greeted the two soldiers, then went on to explain that no one in Germany knew where Mussolini's Italian captors were holding him. However, General Schellenberg suspected that the Italian 'renegades' as Himmler called them, were about to hand the Duce over to the Western Allies. Mussolini would serve as a scapegoat so that the 'renegades' could clear their own consciences.

Now Himmler started to reel off a list of names of people who might be able to help Skorzeny. The latter fumbled in his pocket for his notebook to take them down. 'Are you crazy?' Himmler snapped. 'You can't write these things down. They're top secret. You'll have to memorize them, man.'

Himmler babbled on, before concluding with an order for Skorzeny to find Mussolini as quickly as possible. For 'Italy's defection is certain. It is only a matter of time. There are Italians in Portugal, who are already preparing to begin talks with the Allies.'

Skorzeny then went out to call his adjutant in Friedenthal. While he waited for the call to come through he paced the corridor, smoking a cigarette to calm his nerves. Suddenly a voice snapped behind him, 'So you can't live without cigarettes!'

Skorzeny turned round startled. It was Himmler. 'These eternal cigarettes,' he sniffed disdainfully. 'I can see you're not the right man for the job.' And with that he disappeared as abruptly as he had come.

In the weeks that followed Hitler and the new Italian government under Marshal Badoglio played a double-game, hypocritically assuring each other of their eternal friendship. During this time Canaris and Schellenberg vied with each other to find out where Mussolini was hidden. Twice Canaris gave Schellenberg a false clue. In the end the latter had to protest to Hitler personally. Later Skorzeny, who was doing the searching for Schellenberger, wrote; 'Was Canaris really interested in carrying out the aim of the German High Command?' Obviously Skorzeny didn't think he was.

While Himmler consulted astrologers, clairvoyants and fortune-tellers, Skorzeny finally found that the Italians were holding Mussolini captive in a hotel in the high peaks of the Gran Sasso, one hundred miles from Rome as the crow flies. On the same day Eisenhower announced that peace had been signed between Italy and the Western Allies.

The start of the great rescue operation had been planned for dawn, but the gliders which were to carry Skorzeny's rescue team to the top of the mountain were delayed on the Riviera. He cursed at the news but consoled himself with the thought that, by the time they arrived, the Italian guards would have eaten a heavy lunch and be inclined to take a siesta. At least they wouldn't be as alert as they should have been.

In the meantime, Skorzeny's trusted adjutant, Captain Radl, formerly of the Brandenburgers, had picked up in Rome the pro-German Italian General Soletti, whom he bustled into a car, telling him that he was needed for 'an important enterprise'. Skorzeny needed him to prevent 'any unnecessary shedding of blood'.

Finally, at noon, the twelve gliders were drawn up, ready for lift-off. Suddenly the wail of the air-raid sirens shattered the air. Twin-engined Allied bombers came in low, winging their way across the field at three hundred miles an hour. As bombs tumbled from their bellies Skorzeny and his men scattered. The attack lasted fifteen minutes, while Skorzeny prayed that at least a couple of the gliders would be spared. But when the raid ended he was relieved to see that not a single one of them had been hit.

At one o'clock the little armada took off. Skorzeny was in the second flight of gliders with Soletti crouched between his legs. Almost immediately the first flight was lost in a cloud bank (they never made it). But Skorzeny was too concerned with the heat inside the plane to notice. 'I suddenly noticed,' he recalled, 'that the corporal behind me was being sick and the General in front had turned green. . . . Flying obviously didn't agree with them.'

He also realized that the pilot was flying blind, relying on Skorzeny's knowledge of the Gran Sasso – he had flown over the place already – to guide them. But he couldn't see through the glider's thick celluloid windows. Then the voice of the pilot towing the glider came over the intercom. 'Regrets, but flights one and two are no longer ahead of us. Who's to take over the lead now?'

'This was bad news,' Skorzeny recollected. 'What had happened to them? At that time I did not know that I had only seven machines instead of nine behind me. Two had fallen foul of a bomb crater right at the start.'

But Skorzeny didn't reveal his uneasiness to the tow pilot. He replied, 'We'll take over the lead ourselves.' Seizing his knife he carved a hole in the glider's canvas. Fresh cool air rushed in. The General's colour turned from green to normal.

A little while later Skorzeny spotted his objective: the valley of the Aquilla far below. 'Helmets on,' he commanded and the men prepared for action. The fortress-like hotel where Mussolini was being held came into view perched on the top of a mountain. 'Slip the towrope,' Skorzeny ordered.

A sudden silence. No sound save the rush of the wind under their wings. Slowly the pilot of the glider swung it round in a lazy circle. Skorzeny searched for the landing strip which he had already noted on his first flight over the place. There it was – a triangular patch of grass scrub.

The landing strip was terribly steep and littered with boulders. But there was no turning back now. The glider started to dive sharply, 'Crash landing!' Skorzeny yelled. Then, for the pilot's information, he cried, 'Get as near to the hotel as possible.' He tensed his body for the crash to come.

At the last moment Lieutenant Meyer, the pilot, released the parachute brake. The frail wooden plane lurched forward and hit the stony ground hard. It slithered forward, canvas and wood ripping and splitting, trailing a huge wake of dust behind it. One last mighty heave and they skidded to a stop. They had made it in one piece.

Skorzeny followed the first man out. They were within fifteen metres of the entrance to the hotel. Above them a lone Italian soldier was gaping at this unexpected arrival from the sky, but

Skorzeny didn't give him time to sound the alarm. He doubled forward, machine pistol like a toy in his sledgehammer of a fist. '*Mani in alto!*' he bellowed. The Italian's hands shot upwards like an express lift. Skorzeny charged through the door. Behind it another Italian soldier was crouched over a radio set. Skorzeny kicked the man's chair from under him and the Italian fell to the floor. Then Skorzeny brought the butt of his weapon down on the radio and smashed it.

He ran on. Before him a three-metre wall loomed up. One of his men raced forward, bent his back and offered it to Skorzeny. Skorzeny clambered on it and over the wall. The rest followed. Skorzeny, panting hard now, faltered. Above him, looking down, was that well-remembered heavy-jawed faced and completely bald head. It was the Duce!

'Away from the window,' he cried, knowing that the Italian guards had been ordered to kill Mussolini if any attempt at escape was made. The Duce disappeared at once.

Skorzeny's men rushed into the hotel lobby. They collided with a mass of cursing, frightened Italian soldiers, struggling to find their helmets and weapons. Skorzeny cut right through them. One of his sergeants booted the tripod of a machine gun that the Italians were trying to set up. It slithered across the highly polished floor.

Skorzeny clattered up the grand stairs. He bumped into two young Italian officers. Behind them he saw Mussolini's deathly pale face once again. Skorzeny hesitated. One of his officers, a Lieutenant Schwerdt, came running up. Suddenly both officers grinned. Two smiling faces beneath the rimless helmets of the German paratroopers had appeared at the window behind the Italians. His men had shinned up the hotel's lightning conductor!

Slowly the Italian officers raised their hands. They knew when they were beaten. *In exactly four minutes Skorzeny had rescued the man who was being sought not only by the two German intelligence services but also those of Britain and the United States!*

Mussolini was unshaven and deathly pale, dressed in a crumpled, unpressed blue-grey suit. He didn't look at all like the man the Roman mob had once adored and cheered. But there was no mistaking the joy in the Duce's eyes when he realized that he was being rescued.

Skorzeny was well aware of the importance of this historic

moment. He clicked his heels together and stretched out to his full height. 'I have been sent by the Führer to set you free, Duce,' he announced formally.

Mussolini, a man who had always had an eye for the dramatic moment, responded in kind. 'I knew that my friend Adolf Hitler would not leave me in the lurch,' he declared and then he reached up and brought Skorzeny's head down so that he could embrace him.

An hour later Mussolini was on his way to Vienna, freed from one kind of captivity by his 'friend Adolf Hitler', only to enter another more subtle kind which would end with his assassination.

For Skorzeny it was a time of great personal triumph.* He was awarded the Knight's Cross of the Iron Cross by Hitler, given an engraved gold watch by Mussolini, which from now onwards when asked the time, he would always say, 'I'll just refer to Mussolini time'. Even Churchill showed grudging admiration, saying in the House of Commons, 'The stroke was one of great daring and conducted with a heavy force. It certainly shows there are many possibilities of this kind open in modern war.'

It did. Unwittingly Skorzeny had shown the military world a new way of conducting war. What the British had tried and failed to do in 1941 when they had sent a party of commandos to kidnap or kill Rommel, Skorzeny had pulled off. Now military planners realized that armed conflict had been extended into the area of such gangster methods as kidnapping and assassination. The way ahead was clear and, indeed, within the year two young officers of the British SAS would kidnap a German general on the island of Crete and spirit him back to Egypt. Churchill had learned Skorzeny's lesson exceedingly quickly, it seemed.

While Skorzeny was fêted and allowed by Hitler to recruit a special commando battalion for similar missions on every front that the Germans were fighting, Schellenberg put the final touches to his secret dossier on the Canaris betrayal. It started with Canaris's attempts to warn the West in 1940, went on to his traitorous contacts with the Swiss a year later and ended with his current dealings with the Italians.

Finally he presented Himmler 'with a dossier which included absolute proof of Canaris's treachery'. It ended with the sentence,

---

* General Student never forgave Skorzeny for hogging all the limelight. 30 years after the event he was still complaining about the matter to this author.

74

written in Schellenberg's neat lawyer's hand, 'It would have been better for Admiral Canaris to have concerned himself with his own tasks in Italy, rather than carrying on such sessions with Amé.'

The days of the *Abwehr* chief were numbered.*

* By now Canaris had lost virtually all control over the Brandenburgers. Now Skorzeny's SS commandos would make the running. But they did have one final success in the last combined air-land-sea attack of the German forces in the Second World War when they helped to recapture Rhodes and Samos from the British. Their plans succeeded in capturing the English general in command and forced the surrender of 3,000 British troops. It was the last German success in the Mediterranean.

Five: Operation Long Jump
1943

---

*'The only preventive measure one can take
[against assassination] is to live irregularly –
to walk, to drive and to travel at irregular
and unexpected times. . . . As far as possible,
whenever I go anywhere by car, I go off
unexpectedly and without warning the police'*

Adolf Hitler

'Bring in the Jew,' Himmler ordered.

The adjutant opened the door and shouted, 'Bring in the French Jew.'

The two concentration camp guards, rifles slung over their shoulders, appeared immediately. Between them trudged the prisoner in his striped pyjama-like uniform. His skinny face mirrored his surprise at being so suddenly taken from the squalor of the concentration camp to this opulent Berlin HQ. He was a short, skinny man. Once he had been fat. Now the camp uniform hung from his tortured body. His face was pale, hollow and wary. But there was no mistaking the glow in his eyes. They radiated some kind of inner energy. But since he had been seized in Paris, with thousands of other Jews, by the French gendarmes and handed over to the Germans, he had learned to keep his gaze lowered.

For a moment Himmler scrutinized the prisoner. Then he said, 'I hear you speak our language. You may sit there.' He indicated the chair on the other side of his big desk. The prisoner lowered himself very hesitantly on to the black leather seat, as if he half-expected it to be red-hot. Then Himmler opened the big silver cigar box in front of him. 'You will have a cigar?' He clicked his fingers and one of the guards fished out his cigarette lighter and offered the little Jew a light.

Himmler allowed the prisoner a first cautious puff at the expensive cigar before saying, 'Jean-Jacques Beguin, you are a Frenchman and a Jew. We cannot, therefore, expect you to be a champion of the National Socialist cause.'

The prisoner kept his head down. *What was going on?*

'Now I hear,' Himmler continued, 'that you were once a famous hypnotist and mind-reader before our authorities in France – er – apprehended you.' Himmler waited for Beguin's reaction.

'*Jawohl, Reichsführer,*' Beguin answered in heavily accented German. 'In France, and also in Germany. I performed here in Berlin at the *Wintergarten* and *Kroll's* in the thirties before ...' He didn't complete the sentence.

Himmler nodded. 'Yes, I see. I have your file here. We know all about you. Now I'm going to ask you to perform for me. Not for money, nor for fame, but for your life. Do you understand?'

Beguin nodded, still not raising his head.

'If you help us, we shall release you and send you to a neutral country of your choice. You understand I have the power to do this?'

'*Jawohl, Reichsführer,*' Beguin repeated dutifully. There was a chance, then. Of course he didn't trust Himmler or any of these Nazi swine, but the longer he could stay alive, the better chance he had of escape. The alternative was a return to Sachsenhausen and a quick trip 'up the chimney', as his fellow prisoners called the death ovens.

With a nod of his head Himmler indicated that the two guards should go out. The fewer people who knew about this strange affair the better. The adjutant, however, remained. Then Himmler began to speak, but in such a low voice that Beguin had to strain to hear him. 'Listen, Frenchman, several very important persons are about to meet somewhere in the near future, perhaps in a few weeks, perhaps in a month or so. You tell me now where and when that meeting is to take place.'

Softly Beguin said, 'In order to know about that meeting, *Reichsführer*, I need to know some details first.' Knowing that Himmler was a great believer in astrology, he added, 'After all, even an astrologer cannot give an accurate horoscope without knowing the subject's date of birth.'

'Yes, I see, what you mean,' said Himmler, but he did not volunteer any further information.

Beguin went on, 'Naturally under certain conditions, I can find out who these important persons are, if you would allow me to read your mind, *Reichsführer*'.

Himmler kept silent as if considering the matter. Beguin's mind raced. He was being treated royally. But why? Because the people in question were very important. So were they German? If they were, what kind of Germans would they be? Obviously not friends of Himmler or he wouldn't need to ask. Were they some kind of conspirators, plotting against Himmler or Hitler? Perhaps they weren't German at all.

Then Himmler said, 'You may try to read my mind.'

Beguin felt his old authority rise. 'I demand absolute silence,' he replied. 'I would like you to concentrate as hard as you can. I shall now try to read your thoughts.'

Silence descended upon the office. Beguin felt a bead of sweat trickle down the small of his back. He realized that this was going to be the most important minute of his life. His first words might well decide his fate. Then it came to him, 'De Gaulle'. Surely it had to be the rebel French general now in exile in London? He said the name out loud. Himmler sat up. Beguin felt he had hit the bull's eye. But at the door the adjutant grunted scornfully, 'Well, he would say that, *Reichsführer*.'

Beguin reacted as decisively as he had always done on the stage when he had been in a tight corner. De Gaulle was an enemy of the Reich, but it was other enemies of the Germans that Himmler was after. 'Churchill,' he said out of the blue.

As always, he wondered whether he did really have genuine psychic powers. But he'd hit the nail on the head, he could see that. Who could Churchill conceivably meet who was of importance to the Nazi boss? Stalin? Churchill? The arch right-winger wouldn't want to meet the communist dictator. Roosevelt, the US President? He took a calculated risk. 'Roosevelt,' he announced.

Himmler remained silent. Beguin sweated. Why didn't he show some sort of reaction? He took one last desperate gamble. 'Churchill will also meet Stalin,' he ventured.

Himmler's reaction was explosive. He sprang to his feet and yelled, 'Bravo! You have got all three names right. You have done well, Jew. You now have my full confidence and I am prepared to use you further.'

'*Danke, Reichsführer*.'

'You will be taken to an apartment here in Berlin. Thereafter you will attend other sessions here till we can find out all we need to know about this celebrated meeting. You will be provided with food and drink. Women, if you need them, though of course they can't be German women. A matter of racial purity. You will say nothing of these matters to anyone you may meet – on pain of death.'

Minutes later Beguin was outside again, driving through the crowded streets in a big black car. But he saw and heard nothing. His mind was too full. What was going on? What was so important about this meeting of the Allied leaders? Where was it to be held? What were the Germans up to?*

The first clue that the Allied leaders were going to meet to plan the end-strategy of the war was picked up by the German service tapping the undersea cable linking Britain and America. It didn't take a crystal ball for the listeners to know who was the 'Uncle Joe' to whom Roosevelt and Churchill referred. It wasn't much harder for them to discover what the code-names 'Eureka' and 'Carlo Three', where the 'family reunion' would be held, meant. Both referred to Tehran, the capital of Allied-occupied Iran, where the three Allies were in daily contact with one another. Now with the aid of people like Beguin, paid informers and anti-British Iranians, the joint forces of the *Abwehr* and Skorzeny's *Jagdkommando* knew when that 'family reunion' was to be held. They were intent on being present too. Not to acclaim the Allied leaders, nor even to spy on them. They were going to be there to murder them!

After the summer of 1943 Hitler, who up to now had refused to allow any leading Allied personality to be assassinated, began seriously considering the murder of the heads of Allied states. The success of Skorzeny's Italian mission had led him to believe that a handful of daring young men in the right spot could achieve more than armies. Already the Brandenburgers had recruited renegade Russians, mostly deserters from the Red Army, to kill Stalin. Well supplied with funds etc., they had been dropped miles behind the Russian lines. Mostly they had disappeared without being heard from again.

The *Abwehr*, perhaps unknown to Canaris, had dropped two bodies of supposedly British officers over Yugoslavia. The *Abwehr* agents had hoped that the partisans fighting the Germans there in the high mountains would take the bodies to the British

* Jean-Jacques Beguin later hypnotized his guard and escaped. He crossed the frontier to Switzerland in a stolen German uniform and reported to the British Consulate. But no notice was taken of his strange meeting with Himmler and what the latter had wanted to find out from him.

military mission attached to Tito's HQ. The plan was that the bodies would be carrying letters for Tito, all of which were booby-trapped with high explosive. The plan had failed because the partisans had looted the bodies immediately for the cigarettes they had been carrying with them. A packet of twenty Players exploded and half a dozen partisans had been killed.

Now, however, Hitler wanted a more serious operation carried out which would eliminate his three most dangerous enemies at one stroke – Stalin, Churchill and Roosevelt. The discovery that the three Allied leaders were to meet in Tehran some time in November perhaps December seemed to Hitler to offer an ideal opportunity.

Security was poor in Tehran (a certain General Schwarzkopf, father of 'Stormin' Norman' was in charge of the Iranian gendarmerie), many of the tribes were pro-German and, if they weren't, they were only too eager to accept German gold and arms. And there were already German agents in place.

The task of masterminding the plan, which later became codenamed 'Operation Long Jump', was given to Walter Schellenberg of the SD, one of the 'intellectual gangsters of the Third Reich' as Walter Shirer called them. Schellenberg was an ideal choice for the job. He had no moral scruples whatsoever. In his years as Heydrich's pupil, he had indulged in much blackmail and kidnapping. He had not joined the National Socialists out of conviction but from the belief he could make a career out of the 'movement'.

Just like Canaris, with whom he rode daily in Berlin's parks, he had been smitten by that fatal disease of espionage. In his post-war memoirs he wrote with scarcely concealed pride:

'Microphones were hidden everywhere, hidden in walls, under the desk, even in one of the lamps so that every conversation and every sound [in his Berlin office] could be recorded. . . . My desk was like a small fortress. Two automatic guns were built into it which could spray the whole room with bullets. All I had to do in an emergency was to press a button and both guns would fire simultaneously. At the same time I could press another button and block every exit. Whenever I was on a mission abroad, I was under standing orders to have an artificial tooth inserted which contained enough poison to kill within thirty seconds if I were captured. To make doubly sure I wore a signet ring in which, under a large blue stone, a gold capsule was hidden containing cyanide.'

In short, Schellenberg was like a character who could have stepped from one of those Hollywood grade-B movies, set in some obscure Central European country, and directed by one of those heavy-handed refugees from Nazi Germany, which were popular in the mid-forties. A man like this, drugged by the sheer fantasy of his chosen world, in which nothing could be taken at face value, would not be deterred by the enormity of what Hitler had ordered him to do: murder the three most important men in the world. Perhaps Schellenberg never even fully realized the implications of what he was about to do.

But his partner in crime, Admiral Canaris, did. Why did he go along with the younger man's scheme? Was it because he hoped that in this way he might be able to reinstate himself in Hitler's favour? Did he believe that in this way he might really contribute to the successful outcome of Germany's war? Or was it fear of what would happen to him if he disobeyed?

2

Early on the afternoon of 26 July, 1943, Schellenberg and Ernst Kaltenbrunner, Heydrich's successor, met Canaris and one of his new section heads, Colonel Hansen, in the bar of Berlin's Eden Hotel to discuss 'Operation Long Jump'. Schellenberg was his usual charming self. He always aimed at winning any argument in five minutes, 'as if,' as one observer noted, 'he were asking you how you liked Walter Schellenberg.' Then, 'if he encountered opposition he showed himself capable of suddenly giving way. With a disarming smile he started yielding to his opponent's point of view, capitulating on terms which he tried to negotiate fairly and gently.'

On this July day, while Kaltenbrunner dosed himself morosely with *Kognak* and said little, Schellenberg was particularly charming to Canaris because he needed the latter's help if the new operation was going to be successful. Canaris already had a team on the ground in Iran. Under the command of a Brandenburger, Major Schulze-Holthus, a small group of Germans had rallied a large number of tough tribesmen around them.

Not long before one of Schellenberg's own teams had parachuted in for the coming operation under the command of SS *Hauptsturmführer* Kurmis, who had told Schulze-Holthus curtly, 'it is out of the question that an SS formation should be commanded by a *Wehrmacht* officer. Compared with the SS, *Wehrmacht* officers are only second-rate citizens.'

Schulze-Holthus had looked at his shaggy-haired, hook-nosed bodyguard of tribesmen who dominated the wild Baarmi-i-Firuz Mountains and snapped back, '*Hauptsturmführer*, for this insubordination I could legitimately have you shot on the spot by my bodyguard.'

That had ended the question of who was in command in Iran.

At the end of the Eden Bar meeting the two agreed to co-operate on Operation Long Jump, but still nothing much happened, save that Canaris promised he could put the mob on the streets of Tehran for the day of the planned assassination. This would stretch to full capacity Schwarzkopf's ability to protect the Big Three.

July gave way to August and, under pressure from Himmler, Schellenberg called another conference at Gestapo HQ in Prinz Albrechtstrasse on 14 August, 1943. By now the Germans knew that de Gaulle was not going to be at the Tehran conference, but as they had set up four assassination teams, one for each Allied leader, they decided to merge the *Abwehr*'s and the SS's teams, with preference being given to those men already under training who spoke English and Russian.

The project began to shape up. The men, after completion of their training, would be paradropped into the Baarmi-i-Firuz mountains, where Major Schulze-Holthus would ensure that they had a secure base for the operations in Tehran.

In the meantime, in Iran, Allied counter-intelligence was preparing to prevent any attempt on the Big Three's lives. Stalin, for instance, refused to attend the conference unless the British provided air cover from the Russian border to Tehran. The Soviet dictator was afraid his plane might be attacked by German suicide squads. The British promised a whole squadron of Spitfires to ensure his plane arrived safely. Even so, Beria, his police chief, pumped whole battalions of secret police into the Iranian capital.

The British and the Americans didn't lag far behind. They already had scores of agents in Tehran, watching not only Iranian nationalists and German sympathizers, but also Russian agents. As George Greenfield, an observer at the conference, wrote later, 'Every cafe had its quota of spies. There were always sad-looking men who never removed their overcoats, hunched over empty cups of coffee or fondling a glass of *arak* by the hour. They might be paid by CICI [Combined Intelligence Centre, Iran] to spy on the Russians and German agents, or paid by the Germans to spy on the Allies – or paid by the American OSS to spy on everybody.'

It was all a little like a continental comic opera. But it had serious undertones. The British Legation, for instance, where the Big Three would meet to celebrate Churchill's birthday, was a security man's nightmare. Determined assassins could have scaled the compound's wall anywhere and there was only a single company of the Buffs, plus a few policemen, to guard the sprawling place. If the Big Three were going to be assassinated anywhere, it would be at the British Legation. The Soviet Embassy was heavily guarded and Roosevelt never went anywhere without being surrounded by Secret Service agents, toting machine guns. More than once they had elbowed Churchill, who was guarded by a *single* Scotland Yard detective, out of the way in their eagerness to protect their President. Churchill had taken it all in high good humour.

But although the German plotters knew by now that the Allies were aware that something was afoot, they continued their preparations for the assassination. More agents were dropped into Iran. A gang of weight-lifters, a traditional Persian sport, were recruited to cause a distraction in Tehran when the time was ripe. Iranian tribesmen would help to seal off the exit and entrance routes into the capital and disrupt Allied traffic. Bit by bit the plan was falling into shape.

But there was still the question of who should lead the assassination attempt. Schellenberg and Himmler thought they knew the answer. It could be no one else but Skorzeny, who had just pulled off the Mussolini rescue. Now Skorzeny, with two battalions of Brandenburgers and SS men from the 'Hunting Commando', was in position outside Vichy in France. The plan was to kidnap Marshal Pétain, the head of the Vichy French rump state, in case he tried to do a deal with the Western Allies, and take him to Germany as a hostage for France's good behaviour.

After the war Skorzeny was reluctant to discuss the assassination project for obvious reasons. His reputation was bad enough as it was. In his memoirs he devotes just one page to the

'Iranian affair', as he called it, stating, 'Fortunately a Junkers 290 carrying a team for Persia was prevented from starting by an accident.'

Because the chief German Iranian agent disappeared, 'I rejected the whole plan. ... After I rejected the plan, they turned in all probability to Canaris, but they never told me anything about it.'*

Skorzeny's excuse for getting out of this operation, which, if it had succeeded, would have made him the most famous man in Germany, and the most infamous internationally, is pretty threadbare. He had realized after Stalingrad and El Alamein that Germany was losing the war. He could imagine his fate after an Allied victory if he were in any way connected with an attempt to murder the Big Three.

So, after the need to kidnap Pétain vanished, he took himself off to Yugoslavia. Life was dangerous there, but not as dangerous as it might be if the Allies won the war. His self-imposed mission was to take the Partisan leader Tito 'dead or alive'.

There he toured the country, following various rumours as to where Tito's HQ was located. Finally it was pinpointed in the mountains near Zagreb. Driving a Mercedes, he set off for the Croatian capital. The local German commander discouraged him; 'You'll never make it. There hasn't been a Mercedes down this road in a year. As soon as your car is spotted, the word will be passed and Tito's men will be waiting for you.'

But he made it. In Zagreb he tried to 'borrow' a couple of companies for the attack on Tito's HQ. He would dress them as partisans and make a surprise assault on the caves in which Tito had his headquarters. But the German general in command wasn't allowing anyone to 'borrow' his precious infantry. So Skorzeny returned to the Reich, tail between his legs.

Meanwhile Operation Long Jump fizzled out ignominiously in November, 1943. The only excitement at the Tehran Conference was provided by an unknown private of the 'Buffs'. One evening Churchill and his Foreign Minister, Anthony Eden, were returning to the Legation three sheets in the wind when they were challenged by the sentry of the East Kents. Churchill growled in that famous voice, which everyone was imitating in those days, 'I

---

* Twenty years ago, in conversation with the author, Skorzeny stubbornly refused to be drawn on the subject of Tehran.

am the Prime Minister.' The sentry, thinking his leg was being pulled by some drunk, yelled, 'Fuck off!'

Happily Churchill didn't take the incident too seriously and the private remained unpunished. But for many years the private told the story of how he, a humble private, had once told Churchill to 'fuck off'.

3

'Operation Long Jump' was the last major operation in which Canaris was involved. Three months later his luck ran out at last. On 18 February, 1944, Hitler ordered that the *Abwehr* should be dissolved as a separate organization and its members, including what was left of the Brandenburgers under Canaris's command, be merged into General Schellenberg's Security Service.

The road to Canaris's dismissal had started at what later became known in Schellenberg's circle as 'Frau Solf's Tea Party'. On 10 September, 1943, while Operation Long Jump was in full swing, Frau Solf, the widow of the former German Ambassador to Japan and a convinced anti-Nazi, had given one of her celebrated '*Kaffee und Kuchen*' teas for distinguished people of like mind with herself. Her guests contained such illustrious people as Bismarck's granddaughter, Countess Hanna von Bredow, and Elizabeth von Thadden, a famous headmistress, who had brought along with her a handsome young protégé of Swiss nationality, Dr Reckse, who worked in Berlin's celebrated la Charité Hospital.

Dr Reckse, being neutral, presumably did not need to curb his tongue as much as the Germans present. He expressed bitterly anti-Nazi sentiments, in which the others, encouraged by his outspokenness, joined. Especially eloquent was a Dr Otto Kiep, a high German Foreign Office official, who had been dismissed from his post as German Consul General in New York for having attended a dinner in the honour of the Swiss Jew, Albert Einstein.

Long before the party was over Dr Reckse had volunteered to take letters to the group's anti-Nazi friends in Switzerland, as well as British and American diplomats there. In short he was encouraging these upper class Germans to commit high treason. Thereupon, the little party ended in a jolly round of hand-shaking and kisses on the cheek in the continental fashion before Dr

Reckse hurried away with the precious letters to Schellenberg's office at No 10 Prinz Albrechtstrasse. Reckse was, naturally, a Gestapo spy!

Himmler, Schellenberg and Gestapo Mueller were overjoyed but they didn't arrest the group of traitors at once. They wanted to give them more rope to hang themselves. But they had not reckoned with a spy among spies. The German Resistance had tapped Dr Reckse's phone and had learned of the plot. Kiep was informed. He passed the word on to other guests at the party and to all other associates whom he thought might be implicated.

The frightening news of the impending arrests by the Gestapo spread week by week, from city to city, indeed right over Germany's borders until the information finally reached Istanbul. Here two of Kiep's closest friends heard they might be recalled for questioning. They were Erich Vermehren and his beautiful aristocratic wife, Elizabeth von Plattenberg. Both were *Abwehr* agents.

For a while the two of them waited and wondered what to do. Then they heard that most of the Solf group had been arrested, tried in secret and executed on 12 January, 1944. Now they knew what was in store for them if the Gestapo got its hands on them.

They hesitated no longer. They knew who the representative of the British Secret Service was in Istanbul. They got in touch with him and offered, in exchange for safety, to tell him what they knew – and they knew plenty. Within forty-eight hours the British had flown the Vermehrens to Cairo and from there to London. The great scandal had broken.

The defection of the Vermehrens was the last straw for Hitler. The *Abwehr* had failed to find Mussolini. Canaris had also reassured him that Italy would stay in the war on Germany's side. Now this. At first it was thought, mistakenly, that the Vermehrens had absconded with the *Abwehr* codes (in fact, the British Ultra team had cracked the *Abwehr* codes years before). Now this defection, plus the arrests of General Oster and von Dohnanyi for high treason, convinced Hitler than the *Abwehr* was rotten to the core. On 18 February, 1944, he ordered that the *Abwehr* should be dissolved as a separate institution. Those agents and Brandenburgers still under command and regarded as loyal should be placed at the disposal of Kaltenbrunner and Schellenberg.

Surprisingly Canaris was not arrested. He was not even retired, as Himmler expected he would be (though Himmler still protected him against the attacks of his more aggressive underlings such as Kaltenbrunner and Mueller). Instead he was actually given a new post, not a very important one, but a job all the same. He became Chief of the Office for Commercial and Economic Warfare.

As former SD agent, Wilhelm Hoettl, said after the war, 'It seems astonishing that Canaris could have succeeded in retaining his position until as late as February, 1944, in spite of the fact that his political views remained by no means unknown and that his organization had been so widely discredited in the eyes of the Nazi regime.'

Indeed, right to the end of his ten-year stint as head of the *Abwehr*, Canaris remained a mysterious figure. The Gestapo and SD files on him ran to several volumes. The men who hated or envied him his position already had enough on him to hang him. Yet always they stayed their hand.

Only a few months before, Kaltenbrunner had gone to Himmler with fresh evidence of Canaris's treachery. But Himmler had said that he knew all about Canaris and he had good reasons of his own for not taking action against him. Kaltenbrunner had gone away puzzled.

Once Heydrich had said of Canaris, half in admiration, half in warning, 'He's an old fox whom you've got to watch'. Now the old fox wandered off to his new job with its empty title. Everywhere else his agents were surrendering to the Allies while there was still a chance. Others waited tensely for that early morning knock on the door which would herald the arrival of the leather-coated men of the Gestapo.

Meanwhile the Canaris dossiers were put away in Schellenberg's safe, while the triumphant young general got on with organizing his new outfit. Still, Schellenberg was realist enough to know that he hadn't heard the last of Canaris and those who plotted against Hitler's life. Then out would come that incriminating dossier. Canaris had just one more year to live.

Six: Operation Rocket-Launcher
1944

'With a sabre, you always go for the head, my friend.'

Otto Skorzeny

On 10 September, 1944, Skorzeny was invited to Hitler's HQ. After a long and tiring day of briefings, he was invited to stay that evening for a less formal gathering. With Field Marshal Keitel, Colonel-General Jodl, Foreign Minister Ribbentrop and Himmler, he took his place in one of the easy chairs and listened to a somewhat sardonic lecture by Hitler on the situation on the Eastern Front.

Finally, Hitler, still shaky from the bomb attack the previous July, got round to the subject of Germany's major ally in the East, Hungary. He said, 'We have secret information that the Hungarian Regent, Admiral von Horthy, is attempting to meet the enemy to achieve a separate peace for Hungary. That would mean the loss of our armies. Not only is he trying to negotiate with the Western Allies, he is also trying to arrange talks with the Russian leaders.'

That shocked Hitler's audience. Horthy was renowned as an anti-communist. He had brutally put down the communist revolution under Bela Kun after the First World War. If Horthy was negotiating with the communists, things *were* bad.

Hitler looked at Skorzeny. 'So, Skorzeny, in case the Regent does not honour his pledges, you are to prepare for the military occupation of Burgberg.' (He meant the Regent's fortified hilltop home in Budapest.)

Skorzeny thought of the map he had seen earlier that day which showed the number of divisions the Russians had in the Carpathians. If Horthy surrendered, those 120 divisions would slaughter the betrayed German troops in that part of the Eastern Front. Once the flood tide of the Russian advance had been opened, there might not be any means of stopping it till they reached Berlin.

Hitler was still speaking: 'The General Staff has in mind a parachute operation. You are to start preparing for this operation immediately, as the corps staff is just being set up. Now in order that you need not be faced by any difficulties, I am going to give you far-reaching powers.' He nodded to Jodl, his Chief of Operations.

Jodl rose to his feet and swiftly sketched in what Skorzeny was to be given: a squadron of gliders, two battalions of paras and an elite formation made up of battle-hardened officer cadets. In addition he was to be loaned a plane from the Führer's special flight. Thereupon he was handed a paper bearing the golden eagle of the Third Reich and signed by the Führer himself. It conferred far-reaching powers on him. Hitler looked at Skorzeny significantly, 'Remember, Skorzeny,' he said, 'I'm counting on you.'

Thus for a time Skorzeny forgot the special weapons with which he was experimenting, such as the V-2s to be fired at New York from a U-boat, and set about the new task, which was more after his own heart. Single-handed almost, he had, somehow or other, to keep Hungary in the war on Germany's side.

Two days later a certain Dr Wolf from Cologne arrived in Budapest and took up residence in a modest hotel far away from those frequented by German officers. With the aid of a dog-eared Baedeker, he started studying the environs of the Burgberg. Dr Wolf was, in fact, Otto Skorzeny.

At the same time he tried to find out as much as he could about the ageing Regent and his habits. His German sources were often conflicting, but all agreed that the Admiral was very much under the influence of his younger son, Milos Horthy. 'Miki', as he liked to be called, was notorious for his wild life as a playboy and his extravagant parties, but since his older brother Istvan had been killed in action on the Eastern Front he had become the apple of his father's eye.

Skorzeny also learned that the young Horthy had begun to negotiate with the representatives of Marshal Tito and had agreed to surrender Hungary to Russia, for whom Tito was acting as a middleman. Accordingly Skorzeny decided to help the local Gestapo in their plan to capture Miki Horthy the next time he met the Yugoslavians. 'Operation Mickey Mouse', as it was code-named, was under way.

On Sunday 15 October, the young Horthy arranged to meet the Yugoslav negotiators in the second-floor office of a house in an old square near the Danube. So the Germans arranged to take the upper floor of the same house. Once the meeting started, they would break in, while Skorzeny and his commandos moved in on the house from outside.

It was a quiet autumn morning when Skorzeny drove into the square, empty save for two Hungarian trucks parked outside the building where the meeting would take place. A little further off there was a canvas-backed Hungarian Army truck and a sports car which Skorzeny recognized as belonging to the young Horthy. Skorzeny parked opposite and, raising the bonnet of his engine, pretended to be fiddling with it. Behind him a hand reached round the canvas flap at the back of the truck and lifted it cautiously. Skorzeny caught a quick glimpse of three soldiers huddled over a machine gun on a tripod. The Hungarians were obviously prepared for trouble.

So was Skorzeny. A few moments later two German military policemen strolled up. They looked like a routine police patrol. But their look of casual unconcern soon vanished. Before anyone could stop them, they darted into the building.

The Hungarians reacted at once. A soldier pulled back the canvas flap of the truck and a machine gun burst into life. One of the policemen at the door fell to the ground. Skorzeny raced across, grabbed him by the scruff of the neck and dragged him to the cover of his own car. Some Hungarian soldiers who had been 'loitering' in the next street ran forward to join their comrades, but Skorzeny also received reinforcements. Nevertheless things were getting sticky. He was outnumbered by the Hungarians and needed his last reserves quick. He blew three sharp blasts on his whistle. His second-in-command, the former Brandenburger, Baron von Foelkersam, and his men came pelting down the street from their hiding place, firing from the hip as they ran.

The sight of these tough-looking reinforcements took the heart out of the Hungarians. They drew back into a side street, not into the conspirators' house. That was good enough for Skorzeny. At the head of his men he ran for it. Throwing stick grenades and firing off bursts to the left and right, they raced for the entrance.

Then the Hungarians started to fight back again. From the roof of the building, they began dropping slabs of marble and huge pieces of concrete on the running men below. But these did not stop Skorzeny and his commandos. They entered the house and found that the Germans from the upper floor had already captured young Horthy and were holding him captive. But the Regent's son was not taking his capture calmly, so Skorzeny ordered his men to roll him up in a blanket and tie it up with the curtain ropes. In an instant the writhing bundle was tied up and the package was ready.

'To the airfield,' Skorzeny ordered. 'I'll follow.'

He paused while Horthy's friend, Bornesmiza, was also wrapped up. Then the two were carried outside and dumped in the back of a truck. Skorzeny turned to Captain von Foelkersam: 'And no more shooting. Understand?' The younger officer nodded.

The whole action had taken less than ten minutes. Now the question remained: how would Admiral von Horthy take the kidnapping of his only son? Would it have the desired effect of forcing Horthy to remain in the war on Germany's side?

In the hotel which now served as Skorzeny's HQ, he and his officers waited impatiently for Horthy's reaction. After a while they received a telephone call from the German legation saying that the Burgberg had been completely sealed off by troops and tanks. The Hungarians had even laid mines on all the approach roads.

Then Radio Budapest cut into its normal programme to say that listeners should stand by for an important announcement by the Regent. He was timed to speak at two o'clock that Sunday afternoon.

The Admiral began with an angry tirade against his erstwhile German ally. The Germans, he declared firmly, had lost the war. Now Hungary must make its decision. His was to make peace with the Russians and he concluded by saying that he had already drawn up a provisional armistice with the advancing Red Army. Hostilities between the Russians and the Hungarians would cease at once. The kidnapping scheme had failed.

The disappointed Skorzeny was cheered up a little later when told that, with typical Hungarian carelessness, the Regent had forgotten to notify his armies at the front that all hostilities with the Russians had ceased. All his soldiers knew was what they had just heard on Radio Budapest. Some were still fighting the Red Army. Others were reluctant to drop their weapons and allow the Russians through their prepared positions. The thought flashed through Skorzeny's mind that there still might be a chance.

He contacted SS General Bach-Zelewski, a brutal soldier who had recently reduced Warsaw to rubble after the Polish Home Army had risen against the Germans. The General's plan was to blast the Burgberg off the face of the earth with a huge 25-inch mortar that had been used to smash the defences of the Russian fortress of Sebastopol in the early days of the war with Russia.

Skorzeny managed to convince the General that such an action would mean the end of any hope of a German-Hungarian understanding. After some discussion the two decided to throw a cordon from the 22nd SS Panzer Division around the Burgberg and wait a little longer before starting a new operation that Skorzeny had planned – *Unternehmen-Panzerfaust* (Operation Rocket-Launcher).

Again it was a typical Skorzeny action. The leisurely movement of the Panzers would indicate, so Skorzeny hoped, that the Germans were preparing for a long-drawn-out siege of the fortress. Then, at dawn, a couple of sorties would be launched on the Hungarian positions to keep the defenders occupied. During these feints Skorzeny would slip through the Hungarian positions on one of the main roads leading to Horthy's residence, with his men sitting openly in their vehicles as if they were on a routine road march. Once the Hungarians reacted, the mixed bunch of SS men, paras and Brandenburgers would spring into action. The German staff officers shook their heads doubtfully. It was all going to be very risky. The sorties to be carried out by the officer-cadets were to be launched against the steep sides of the fortress where the Hungarians were well dug in. They thought there would be heavy losses. Their main objection was to Skorzeny's 'road march'. If the Hungarians took his defenceless men from the side – one machine gun would suffice – there'd be mass slaughter. Nevertheless Skorzeny insisted that the plan should be carried out as he had conceived it.

Some time that same evening a Hungarian General appeared at the SS HQ. He protested against the appearance of the SS Division at the base of the Burgberg. What were the Germans' intentions? Were they planning military action against their allies?

The Germans retaliated by asking why the German diplomats

were confined to their quarters on the Burgberg and what the Hungarians intended to do with them. The General was non-plussed, which Skorzeny took to mean that he had a conscience and was embarrassed by the recent peace offer to the Russians. Taking advantage of the situation, he suggested that the Hungarians should remove the mines from the Wienerstrasse which led directly to the German Legation. The General said he'd see what he could do. It was now two o'clock in the morning and time was running out.

At three Skorzeny took up his position at the head of his commandos. It was a pitch black night and he had no idea whether the Hungarians had removed the mines or not. For this was the road he was going to use in his dash up the hill. He told his men that he wanted no firing unless it was absolutely necessary. Their task was to drive through the Hungarian positions without a fight. 'After all, the Hungarian soldiers are not our enemies.'

At five-thirty the long column set off. Skorzeny rode in front in an open jeep. Behind him came four tanks, then a troop of Goliaths, small tracked vehicles, packed with high explosive which could be detonated against fortifications by remote control. Bringing up the rear were trucks carrying infantry.

Thirty minutes later they reached the start-line and stopped for a few moments. Skorzeny walked over to his old comrade of the Gran Sarso rescue, von Foelkersam, where the assault troops had assembled.

They said that they were worried about the reaction of the Hungarian tank troops known to be above them on the hill. Otherwise they were confident that they could pull it off.

At one minute to six Skorzeny brought his arm down sharply. It was the signal to start. The men ran back to their vehicles and their engines sprang to life. Operation *Panzerfaust* was under way.

They crawled up the Wienerstrasse where the General had indeed removed the mines. Much relieved, they rolled on. Things were going well. Sentries appeared out of nowhere and clicked to attention at the sight of the Germans. Skorzeny waved to them cheerfully. The sentries obviously had no orders to stop the Germans. Behind him the tank commanders saluted. They were through the first obstacle.

Suddenly from far off there came the crump of explosives, but

98

they kept on. They were approaching the German Legation. Behind it was the road to Horthy's palace. It was straight and not too steep. Skorzeny nudged his driver, who put his foot down hard on the accelerator. The little Volkswagen picked up speed. Behind him the other vehicles did the same. They came to a crossroads. Half the column took a side road, also leading to Horthy's palace. They clattered on. Now Skorzeny knew that the whole Hungarian garrison must have been alerted by the noise of the advancing Germans. Then three Hungarian tanks emerged, having spotted the Germans. But the first tank driver, realizing he was outnumbered, skidded to a halt and his gunner raised his cannon to indicate that he wasn't going to fire. Skorzeny's jeep sped on.

A three-foot-high barrier confronted him. The driver hit the brakes and the jeep skidded to one side. Skorzeny signalled to the Tiger behind him and the driver rushed the barrier. The Tiger rumbled on, only to be faced by six anti-tank guns.

What would the Tiger commander do? Skorzeny didn't wait to find out. In a flash he was out of the Volkswagen. Foelkersam's assault group followed. A bareheaded Hungarian colonel rushed up, pistol in hand, but Foelkersam knocked the pistol out of his hand and they scrambled on.

Another Hungarian colonel came rushing out of the shadows. He skidded to a stop when he saw Skorzeny. 'Lead us to the commandant of Burgberg at once,' he ordered, as if he had the confused situation completely under control. The trick worked and the officer ran on at Skorzeny's side, giving him directions. They crossed a long section of red carpet, then clattered up some stairs. Behind him Skorzeny's men took up a defensive position.

The Hungarian pointed to an ornate door which Skorzeny flung open. A Hungarian soldier lay on a table pushed up against an open window. He was crouched over a machine gun which he was firing into the courtyard below. Skorzeny bellowed an order. Sergeant Holzer pushed by him and tugged the machine gun from the surprised Hungarian's hands and flung it through the window.

Skorzeny saw another door. Later he was surprised by his action now and couldn't find an explanation. For instead of kicking the door in, he *knocked* on it! It was opened after a moment by a Hungarian major-general.

'Are you the commandant of the Burgberg?' Skorzeny asked.

Then, without waiting for an answer, he added firmly, 'I demand you surrender the Burgberg at once. You are responsible if any more blood is spilled. I ask you for an immediate decision.'

There was a moment's silence. From below Skorzeny could hear single rifle shots and the slow chatter of some ancient Hungarian machine gun. 'You can see,' Skorzeny said, 'that all resistance is foolish. I've already taken the castle.'

He guessed that another company of his men under Captain Hunke had by now captured most of the key points in the immediate area. As if summoned by mental telepathy, at that very moment Captain Hunke appeared, his tough face black with powder burns, and reported very formally, 'Yard and main entrance taken without a fight. Request further instructions.'

Skorzeny beamed down at Hunke. He had come at just the right moment. Slowly the Hungarian general said in German, 'I surrender the Burgberg to you and will order the immediate cease fire.' At that juncture Skorzeny and the Hungarian shook hands. Then the major-general went out to give his orders.

Skorzeny moved into another room, which he found full of antagonistic Hungarian officers. But he did not want to humiliate them. Immediately he appointed two of them, both majors, to be his liaison officers. They were to take charge of the surrender of their own men. Skorzeny was naturally aiming at maintaining the fiction that the Hungarians were friends not foes; there had just been an unfortunate misunderstanding.

Then he requested all the officers to follow him into the Coronation Room. Here he addressed them in German. He decided that he had to say something special, laying on the Viennese charm by the spoonful.

'I would like to remind you,' he said in his Austrian accent, which both the Hungarians and the Austrians had in common (most of the officers present had been born when Hungary and Austria had been one under the double eagle), 'that for centuries Hungarians have never fought against Austrians. Always we have been allies. Now there is no reason for difficulties. Our concern is for a new Europe. But this can only arise if Germany is saved.'

As Skorzeny remembered afterwards, 'My Austrian accent obviously supported and strengthened the effect of my words: something which I felt in the pressure of their hands when I shook hands with each one of them afterwards.'

100

Operation *Panzerfaust* was over at the cost of twenty German casualties. Skorzeny's commandos had captured the Burgberg in hours with a handful of men. In the following year it would take the Red Army days and a whole regiment to take the place.

Admiral von Horthy was sent to Germany immediately in a special train to become a 'guest of the Führer' for the rest of the war. At the same time his abdication as Regent was announced. He was replaced by the pro-German Count Scalasi, who cancelled the armistice talks at once.

Now for a couple of days the 'hero of Hungary' took up residence in the palace. Here he lived like 'the king in France', as the German expression has it. He drank the fine Tokay wines from Horthy's cellar, 'entertained' titled and very beautiful women and every evening took his bath in the baroque bath-tub which had once been used by the last Kaiser of Austro-Hungary, Emperor Franz Josef.

Undoubtedly he felt it was a well-earned reward for what he had just achieved. He had kept Hungary in the war. He had saved the German Central Front from being overrun by the Red Army. Now, for the remaining nine months of the war, Hungary would continue to fight on Germany's side.

2

On the afternoon of 21 October, 1944, Skorzeny reported to Hitler's HQ. The Führer welcomed him warmly and exclaimed, 'Well done, Skorzeny. Now sit down and tell me all about Operation Mickey Mouse.'

Skorzeny told his story in detail, making Hitler laugh when he explained how they had wrapped the young Horthy in the carpet. Then, when he was finished and rose to go, Hitler said, 'Stay awhile, I am going to give you the most important job of your life.' His pale face glowed with some of his old energy and enthusiasm. 'In December Germany will start a great offensive. It may decide her fate.'

Hitler said that the Allies expected 'to find a stinking corpse in Germany', but they were in for a surprise. They had won the 'battle of the invasion', only because of their superior air power. That would all change soon. He had picked a time later in the autumn when the skies would be overcast and the Allies would be unable to employ their superior air power.* Besides, by then 'we will have two thousand of the new jet fighters that we have kept in reserve for this offensive.'

This planned offensive, which would become known as the 'Ardennes Offensive' to the Germans, was essentially Germany's last assault in the West, from which, as he explained in detail to Skorzeny, he expected far-ranging political and military gains.

Hitler concluded his exposé with, 'I have told you so much so that you will realize that everything has been considered very carefully and has been well worked out. Now, you and your units will play a very important part in the offensive. As an advance guard you will secure one or more bridges over the River Meuse between Liège and Namur. You will carry out this operation in British or American uniform. The enemy has already played this trick. Only a couple of weeks ago I received a report that Americans wearing German uniform had been active during the fighting in Aachen.'

Hitler paused briefly to let Skorzeny absorb what he had said. Then he continued, 'I know you will do your best. But now to the most important thing. Absolute secrecy! Only a few people know of the plan. In order to conceal your preparations from your own troops tell them that we are expecting a full-scale attack in the area between Aachen and Cologne. Your preparations are intended to be part of the resistance to that attack.'

Skorzeny protested, 'But *mein Führer*, time is short and I have other tasks.'

'Yes,' Hitler agreed. 'I know time is short. But I know you'll do your best. For the period of the offensive I'm sending you a deputy. But one thing, Skorzeny, I do not want you to cross the front personally. You must not run the risk of being captured.'

With that the interview was terminated and Skorzeny left, his head buzzing with ideas and no little apprehension at sending men into battle in enemy uniform. The Brandenburgers had got away with it in 1939/40, but times had changed since then. The war had become more brutalized. Now British commandos and SAS men risked the chance of being shot out of hand if they were captured by the Germans. Skorzeny could guess what would

---

* A secret German weather team was already in the Arctic wastes radioing long-range forecasts back to Germany, specifically for the Ardennes offensive.

happen to any of his commandos caught in enemy uniform. They'd suffer the same fate.

His mood sank even lower when a circular signed by Field Marshal Keitel was brought to his attention. Labelled 'Top Secret', it read: 'To Divisional and Army Commands Only. Officers and men who speak English are wanted for a special mission. Volunteers who are selected will join a new unit under the command of Lt Col Skorzeny to whose headquarters at Friedenthal all applications should be sent.'

Skorzeny raged. A circular of that kind could easily fall into enemy hands with the Anglo-Americans now fighting on Germany's western borders. An Allied Intelligence officer finding it wouldn't need a crystal ball to put the name of the notorious Skorzeny and the requirement for English-speaking troops together and conclude that some kind of covert operation was going to be launched in the West.

But before Skorzeny could really set about training his new outfit, 'Panzerbrigade 150', he was called to an important conference with Himmler at his HQ. Present were Kaltenbrunner, Schellenberg and SS *Obergruppenführer* Pruetzmann, a not very bright Party member who had been running police operations in Russia and Poland before the Red Army had chased him back to the Reich.

Himmler was his usual long-winded self, but finally he took off his pince-nez and said, 'Skorzeny, I want you to take over the Werewolf organization and knock it into shape.'

Himmler now launched into an exposé of the new secret organization of which Skorzeny had not heard before. The idea had been taken from the activities of the Polish Home Army. Schellenberg had formulated plans for a similar organization for Germany, or those parts already occupied by the enemy. When Himmler had first seen the Schellenberg plan, he had snorted, 'This is madness!' But he had soon warmed to it and was currently recruiting five thousand volunteers for the new organization. In essence it would have the task of sabotaging enemy installations, killing top Allied personalities and assassinating Germans who collaborated with the enemy.

Already the Werewolves had their secret passwords, clandestine arms dumps behind enemy lines and all the rest of the material needed for covert operations to be carried out by

Werewolves in civilian dress. Training schools had been established where volunteers from the League of German Maidens, the Hitler Youth and the SS would learn to 'consider it our supreme duty and right to kill, to kill and to kill (as the Werewolf textbook had it), employing every cunning and wile in the darkness of the night, crawling, groping through towns and villages, like wolves, noiselessly, mysteriously'.

Now Himmler wanted Skorzeny to take over, for the *Reichsführer* SS hadn't much faith in the abilities of Pruetzmann, who was then head of this unit. He had a reputation of being lazy and careless. Under other circumstances Skorzeny, who was a born empire-builder, would have jumped at the chance to take over Germany's first resistance organization. But now, racing against time to carry out Hitler's recent instructions, he felt he had no time for additional duties.

Himmler must have seen the look on his face, for he said, 'I know this job would fall within your competence, Skorzeny, but I think you've got enough on your plate for the moment.'

So they compromised. Skorzeny said, 'Certainly, *Reichsführer*, I've more than enough on and I'd like to suggest that I take over all operations outside the border of the Reich.'

Schellenberg breathed a sigh of relief. With Skorzeny out of the running he could wash his hands of the whole stupid affair. As he wrote later, 'I then pointed out to him [Himmler] the senselessness of the Werewolf organization which was now being formed to carry on the struggle. This plan, I said, would bring nothing but further suffering to the German people. Opportunities would arise for every sort of crime to be committed.'

Himmler waved aside his protests, saying merely, 'I'll try to think of some way to finish this business.'

So, for the time being, Skorzeny was allowed to opt out of the preparations for a national German resistance movement. But, unknown to him then, *Werewolf* would furnish him with a new career in the post-war world where no one had much time for the ex-chief of the German commandos.

So Skorzeny returned to the German training base at Grafenwoehr,* Bavaria, where his special force, Panzer brigade 150, was being prepared for the great surprise attack.

* For fifty years after the war it was a training ground for American tank troops.

Seven: The Great Deception 1944

'We shall all meet at the Cafe de la Paix.'

Unknown SS Commando officer to Otto Skorzeny, December, 1944

Lieutenant-Colonel Hermann Giskes was what German soldiers called 'an old hare' – a veteran. But the Colonel's battles had not been fought on the battlefield but in the war in the shadows – espionage. Colonel Giskes was Germany's most successful spy-catcher. In Holland alone he had apprehended fifty agents dropped by parachute by the two English spymasters, Bingham and Blunt, the same Anthony Blunt, art expert and surveyor of the Queen's pictures, who would be revealed long afterwards as a Soviet spy.

When, that February, what was left of the *Abwehr* was merged into Schellenberg's organization Giskes decided he wanted to be as far away from Berlin, from which all the trouble usually came, as possible. He volunteered to work in the espionage field south of the Rhine, coming under the command of Field Marshal Model's Army Group B. Some months later when his old chief Canaris was arrested after the attempt to kill Hitler failed, he felt he had made the right decision. Here, just behind the front, he was left in comparative peace by his superiors in the capital; and it suited him down to the ground. For Colonel Giskes was determined to survive the war, come what may.

In early November, 1944, however, the quiet life he had made for himself in a village just outside Bonn was disturbed by a summons from the headquarters of Field Marshal Model. As he drove he kept a weather eye open for Allied fighter-bombers, which seemed to attack anything that moved in Germany these days, his mood fluctuating between excitement and apprehension. It wasn't every day that an obscure Colonel of Intelligence was summoned to an Army Group HQ.

Model received Giskes personally in a secluded hunting lodge just outside the small town of Munstereifel. Model was small and aggressive, feared by his staff officers on account of his hot temper and respected by his soldiers because he was always at the front. Once, when a company commando had been killed, he'd even led the company back into the attack. There weren't many field marshals like that in the *Wehrmacht*.

As usual he didn't waste time. He asked Giskes at once, 'Can you think of any plan which would fool the Western Allies as to the strategic intentions of my Army Command? It must involve Allied nationals so that it will be entirely convincing.'

At this stage of the war Giskes knew that it wouldn't be easy to find any Allied nationals who would be willing to carry out such a task. He knew that Skorzeny had arranged to have 'sleepers' left behind as the German Army had fled Western Europe two months previously, but these were French, Belgian and Luxembourg citizens who went about their normal business but would work for Germany when the call came. Still it was a problem. He asked Model for four hours to think about it. Model agreed and he left Giskes with his Chief of Intelligence.

The latter gave Giskes a good lunch and then left him to consider what could be done. At three precisely he saw the Chief of Intelligence again. First Giskes made a request. Could he be informed what Army Group B's objective was. By now Giskes had guessed that there was going to be a new offensive in the West.

The Chief of Intelligence was quite adamant. No, he could not disclose any of Model's plans. Giskes had to take his word for it that a great new operative in the West was beyond the planning stage and when it came it would shake the 'Anglo-American bandits' out of their complacency.

Giskes had already read Keitel's circular asking for English-speaking volunteers for Skorzeny's *Jagdkommando* – indeed he had already supplied Skorzeny with captured English plastic explosive, sten guns fitted with silencers, and other equipment – and knew that the *Jagdkommando* would probably fight behind Allied lines in the coming op. 'All right, sir,' Giskes said finally, 'I shall get to work on it immediately. But what if, in preparing a fake cover plan to fool the enemy, by mistake I hit on the real plan?'

Model's Chief of Intelligence was not amused.

Operation Heinrich, as Giskes code-named it, worked well from the start. He had begun with the problem posed by Model: the fake plan had to be conveyed to the Allies by one of their own nationals. His fellow intelligence officers said this was impossible. Who would work for Germany now it was facing defeat? Giskes, who had subverted so many men and women in the last five years, had not been so sure.

In the end he played an old trick often used by spymasters. He would make the man – or men – who were to take the fake plan to the Allies think they were working for some other power than Germany. It was a device the English had used with their working-class agents on the Continent, making them think they were working for Soviet Russia, 'the workers' paradise', when in reality they were spying for plutocratic perfidious Albion.

He approached an engineer of his acquaintance who was currently running a labour camp not far from Germany's border with Luxembourg. Most of the workers were Belgians and Luxembourgers who had become 'honorary Germans' back in 1940. These 'booty Germans', as they were called by native Germans, were allowed out during daylight hours to work under supervision. But the engineer in charge didn't trust them. Most of them would flee at the drop of a hat to their native countries and the engineer knew he had to keep tight control over them.

Naturally the engineer, a loyal German, was horrified when Giskes suggested he should let some of these men escape. Finally he convinced the engineer that the escapers would, unwittingly, help Germany's cause. So Giskes told the engineer his plan. The latter came from Saxony, a province that had been strongly communist before the Nazis had come to power. He should pose as a secret communist, of which there were already many in Germany, for the Soviets were parachuting in agents to revive the old pre-Nazi communist cells. In due course he would approach some of his charges and explain his true sympathies. Then he'd ask the ones he had selected if they would carry secret messages across the border to the Americans if he helped them to escape. The engineer agreed and the scheme was put into motion.

By now Giskes had dreamed up his own great counter-offensive. Surprisingly enough it was very similar to the 'small solution' proposed by some of Hitler's generals. It envisaged a two-pronged attack on the old imperial city of Aachen, which would cut off some ten US divisions. The 'Giskes Plan' – a two pronged attack on Aachen from the direction of Cologne – would fit in with the pre-conceived notions of Allied intelligence officers, who believed an offensive of that kind would explain the supposed presence of the Sixth SS Panzer Army in that area.

Soon the first 'escaper' sneaked out of the camp, aided by the engineer. With him as he 'broke out' he carried a rough sketch of the 'Giskes Plan' and other 'secret details' written on scraps of paper in milk. These were hidden in the lining of an old tobacco pouch. The 'escaper' was instructed to hand the pouch to the first American officer he met. If the Americans wanted any more information they should include in the broadcasts made to Germany from the American-born Radio Luxembourg the phrase 'and regards to Otto from Saxony', the supposed secret communist engineer.

Ten days later, after the first 'slave labourer', as they always called themselves to the Americans, had escaped, the message came through. It gave the old spymaster a certain amount of sardonic pleasure to hear the Radio Luxembourg announcer say, 'And tonight we send regards to Otto from Saxony'.

His ploy had worked. During the rest of November Giskes pulled out all the plugs. More and more Belgians and Luxembourgers managed to escape from the labour camp, working their way easily through the lines because they spoke the same dialect as the German inhabitants of the Eifel. With them they brought ever more information about the 'spoiling attack' which would be 'a Christmas present for the Führer'.

We do not know how much of this information was taken seriously by the Americans, but their intelligence reports of the time are full of references to 'Luxembourg slave labourers who escaped' and 'refugees or escapers from the Bitburg area'.

As for Giskes, he reckoned he could now rest on his laurels. 'By now,' he recalled years later at his retirement home in Bavaria's Rottach-Eggern, 'I knew from my travels in the Eifel that month that something big was happening. Naturally I hoped that I hadn't dreamed up the "real" counter-attack for the unsuspecting Americans, as I had warned Model's Chief of Intelligence I might do. All the same the sight of so many troops, so much armour, so many new guns everywhere made me think of March, 1918 (the last great counter-attack in France in the First World War) and feel a new sense of hope. Perhaps there was a chance for Germany at this late hour after all. So I relaxed, my operation wound up, waiting to see what would happen in the Eifel, looking forward to Christmas, my first in Germany for several years. Little did I know then it would be my last in the Homeland for years to come and under what circumstances I would be spending next Christmas behind bars.'

<h1 style="text-align:center">2</h1>

Now the first of the volunteers started to turn up at Friedenthal from whence they were shipped to Grafenwoehr for further training. They came from all branches of the German service: Merchant Marine, Navy, SS, Army. One of the first to arrive was *Feldwebel* Heinz Rohde, a sharp-faced NCO in his mid-20s. He was recovering from a bad wound and had been on light duties in a signals unit in Hamburg. He was sick of the raids and he thought he was volunteering for a cushy number in the country, away from the almost daily raids on the shattered city. He was soon to change his mind.

After a long journey through Central Germany, Rohde found himself with thirty others, ranging in rank from naval captain to *Luftwaffe* lance-corporal, at the country station of Rappenberg. Here, in the growing darkness, they were met by two SS officers, who told them their mission was top secret. Thereupon they were ordered to give up all their identification documents.

Then they set off on a two-hour ride through the night until they were eventually unloaded at a remote camp guarded by SS men, armed with fixed bayonets. 'They were Ukrainian volunteers, who didn't speak a word of German,' Rohde remembered years later. 'But one thing was clear. Once we passed through the big gate there would be no turning back. We were leaving the real world behind us.'

They certainly were. Almost immediately one of the volunteers was ordered to be shot for giving away the secret. He had sent a letter home, giving a full description of their mission, and it had been intercepted. As he had already sworn on oath not to reveal any details he was ordered to be executed. Isolation was so severe that the sick were not sent to the nearest hospital, but were tended, for better or worse, by the camp's medics. To prevent the usually seasonal colds and flus, all men were inoculated.

Tests were to run to ascertain their degree of competence in English. This proved to be a problem. Most of the volunteers had exaggerated their knowledge of the language. As Skorzeny told his interrogators after the war, 'I had ten men who spoke the English language fluently, thirty or forty who spoke it fairly well and about 150 who managed to make themselves understood only with difficulty.'

Most of these English-speakers were former seamen who had served in the US merchant marines before the war. Some were German-Americans who had lived in the States and possessed dual nationality. A few had served in the US Army, including a handful of turncoats with Nazi sympathies.

The English-speakers were grouped together in a special unit, named after its commander Captain Stielau – 'Gruppe Stielau' – which was kept separate from the rest of Skorzeny's 150 Panzer-brigade. Sergeant Rohde, who was assigned to the Stielau unit, recalled afterwards, 'Almost immediately I was struck by the unusual, almost unsoldierly, attitude of the members of this unit. The tone was easy-going and very comradely, so that in an astonishingly short time we achieved a feeling of togetherness that you usually only find among soldiers in time of great stress at the front.'

The *Stielau* unit started training at once. As Rohde recalled, 'At first we were mostly concerned with learning the idiom of the GIs. The showing of American films, specially war films, played a great role in our training. Then came short visits to American POW camps, where we mixed with the GIs and gained the impression that we were developing into perfect Yankees.'

They learned to lounge like genuine GIs, hands in pockets. They learned how to chew gum and when they lit a cigarette they scraped the match along a wall to do so. They learned how to walk from the hips in the distinctive US fashion.

In December they were broken up into teams, nine in all, who would use American jeeps and American equipment to carry out sabotage, reconnaissance and spying far behind the enemy's lines. They would spread news of disaster, of hordes of Germans advancing. It would be their task to create panic and total confusion behind the American front.

Each jeep would contain four men (which was against US Army regulations. A jeep should only hold three men). They would be the driver, the commander, a saboteur or radio operator and an interpreter, who would do the talking if the jeep was stopped by US troops. He would be the only one in the four-man team who could speak perfect English. But, just in case, every crew member was given the L-pill ('L' for lethal), a phial of prussic acid concealed in the wool of their zippo cigarette lighters. Better suicide, Skorzeny thought, than torture and execution as spies.

In the first days of December, as the volunteers learned the tricks of close combat, sabotage, the use of plastic explosives and the new silenced machine pistols (which had been adapted from the silenced Sten guns which Giskes had given to Skorzeny) the men were introduced to their new identities. As Rohde recalled, 'We were led into the quartermaster's clothing store, which was piled high with all types of American uniform and told to fit ourselves out from underpants onwards. 'Later they were taken into another room and told to pick up suitable identity discs and documents. Rohde thus found himself transformed into Sergeant Morris Wodall of the US Army. 'It was a very funny feeling. Somehow a little eerie, and we lost no time in hiding our American uniforms under the German paratrooper overalls and the little paratrooper cap that went with it.'

With nearly 3,000 men locked away in the remote camp, with their mail strictly censored and their days spent imitating Americans, rumours flew thick and fast. Some said they were going to be dropped in US uniform to relieve the German garrisons which were still holding out in French ports such as Lorient. Others said they were going to launch a surprise attack on the great US cage near Cherbourg, Camp 'Lucky Strike', which held many thousands of German POWs waiting shipment to the United States. A few hinted darkly that there was a much more dangerous mission in front of them – a paradrop into England to help the mass breakout of the quarter of a million German prisoners held there.*

At first Skorzeny tried to kill the rumours. But soon he realized that the rumour-mongers provided vital cover for the real mission. In case one of his men managed to smuggle details outside or a captured man started 'singing', it was better that his

* See C. Whiting: *The March on London* (Leo Cooper, London) for further details.

men believed that the mass of their comrades were going to be employed on a different mission from the real one.

It was about this time that an incident took place which would plague Skorzeny for many years to come. It also resulted in Eisenhower being confined to his own headquarters for days during the crucial phase of the battle to come, guarded by a whole battalion of MPs, with a tank escorting his car whenever he ventured out. One morning a young officer of the Stielau Unit asked to have a private talk with Skorzeny. Very seriously he told Skorzeny when they were alone, '*Obersturmbannführer*, I think I know what the real objective is.'

Skorzeny pricked up his ears. Only two other officers in the whole camp knew the real mission. Had one of them talked? 'The Brigade is to march on Paris and capture Eisenhower's headquarters.'

Skorzeny forced himself not to laugh. 'So, so,' he said with a significant frown.

That seemed to convince the lieutenant that he was on the right track. He said, 'May I offer my co-operation sir? I was stationed in France for a long time and know Paris well. My French is good, too. You can rely on me. This is my plan.'

He then explained how the Brigade would enter Paris from various directions, posing as Americans, taking with them some German tanks which they would claim had been captured at the front and were needed in the rear COMZ for technical inspection. Once in Paris they would meet up for a concentrated attack on Eisenhower's HQ at the Petit Trianon.

Skorzeny pretended to go along with the scheme and mentioned he too knew Paris well. He had often had a drink at the Café de la Paix. With that he dismissed the young officer who would naturally relate his brilliant plan to his comrades. Of course he'd mention the celebrated boulevard cafe. As Skorzeny told this author, he would live to 'regret ever mentioning that damned cafe'. But the Legend of the Cafe de la Paix had been born.

As the Stielau unit started to shake down, Skorzeny was still experiencing difficulties with 150 Panzerbrigade. Hitler had promised him all the equipment he would require to kit out his undercover outfit. Jeeps, he had been told, would be given to him in large numbers.

The reality was very different. Hitherto every German officer in the *Wehrmacht* had seemed to possess one, but on the day that Colonel-General Jodl had issued his order requisitioning them for Skorzeny's Brigade jeeps vanished from the face of the earth. In the end Skorzeny sent out his officers to forage for the prized but elusive jeep. In one case, to their great surprise, they found fifteen hidden in a barn.

It was the same with heavier US vehicles. Skorzeny had asked for twenty US Sherman tanks. All he received were two Shermans, six British Daimler armoured cars and eight White half-tracks. In the end he was forced to add metal to the various parts of the German Panther's hull so that it looked roughly like an American tank. As Skorzeny commented after he had seen the first disguised Panther, 'All I can say is that they might just deceive very young troops, viewed at night and from very far away!'

It was little different with the thousands of US uniforms shipped to Grafenwoehr for his Brigade. There were overcoats by the hundred. But they were of little use because it was known that GIs wore combat jackets in battle. After complaints, the German Quartermaster General did send him a large number of US jackets, but they were all covered with POW triangles and the legend 'KG' (*Kriegsgefangener*, POW) on the back. Skorzeny gave up. He told his men, 'It doesn't matter. You can pick up all you want after the breakthrough.'

Slowly the training came to an end. His men now slouched about, chewed gum relentlessly and, when challenged, replied, 'Go and lay a fucking egg,' in best GI fashion, or 'go and crap in yer cap, buddy'. But there was still one problem that Skorzeny and his instructors could not overcome. What would happen to his men if they were taken prisoner or dressed in American uniform and carrying US identification? Skorzeny told his men that the enemy had already violated the rules of war by parachuting saboteurs and commandos behind German lines and by fomenting partisan warfare in German-occupied countries. That kind of conduct legitimized the wearing of enemy uniform. But it didn't satisfy the troops. So Skorzeny advised them not to engage in combat while they were wearing US uniform. Before they went into action *they were recommended to change into German uniform*!

Of course the suggestion was absurd. It was just a sop to calm the worried men. Already, unknown to them, the special unit had been written off by the German High Command. When Field Marshal von Rundstedt, the nominal commander of the great attack, heard of the formation of 150 Panzerbrigade, he asked his chief of staff, General Westphal, to ask Jodl whether such an operation was 'fully in accordance with international law'.

Jodl replied, 'Since the Field Marshal has raised the problem, we have re-examined the matter. There is no question of any infringement of international law. It is merely a war stratagem, such as the other side has already used on all fronts with much greater frequency than we have. You need, therefore, to have no scruples. Moreover, all the men are volunteers. They are quite aware of the possibility that they may be treated as partisans. They have accepted this. No one has forced them into it.'

The inference was clear. If captured, Skorzeny's men were doomed and the German High Command knew it. As von Rundstedt commented on hearing Jodl's advice, '*Mitgegangen, mitgefangen, mitgehangen*'.*

3

Five-thirty, Saturday, 16 December, 1944. With a tremendous roar one thousand guns opened up all along the German front facing General Troy Middleton's 8th Corps. Out of the freezing darkness thousands of German infantrymen started to advance on the positions of the surprised American infantry. There had been warnings enough that the Germans were going to attack here, but General Eisenhower had decided, for reasons of his own, to ignore them.† Now Middleton's 8th Corps began to pay the price for his cruel strategy.

Almost immediately, as the Germans swamped the US front line positions, troops started to pull back, with or without orders. By dawn, with the first snow of the year starting to fall, the roads to the rear were clogged with US troops 'bugging out'. Behind them, or even with them, came the *Stielau* four-man teams in their captured jeeps.

One such team, led by Sergeant Rohde, was heading for the

* 'Gone with, caught with, hanged with'.
† See: C. Whiting: *The Last Assault* for further details of Eisenhower's plan in the Ardennes.

River Meuse. Carefully, obeying all traffic instructions, the Rohde team worked its way through St Vith, heading for Vielsalm and then on through Werbomont to the Meuse. 'Snowdrops', as the Germans called the American military policemen on account of the white-painted helmets they wore, were everywhere. But they were not looking for Germans, yet. They were out for US deserters – and there were plenty of them running away from the crumbling front.

It was an ideal cover for the four Germans of the Rohde team. All the same, the flood of men and equipment moving to the rear slowed them considerably. They had hoped to be able to reconnoitre the Meuse bridge at Huy, the key objective of SS *Obersturmbannführer* Jochen Peiper's Battle Group of the 1st SS Panzer Division, by two in the afternoon. Now, with delay after delay, it was long after two and already beginning to get dark.

Now came a shock for the Germans. The fleeing Americans were driving with their headlights full on. Rohde's driver discovered to his horror that his headlights were almost blacked out, with only two slits kept free for the light to escape. There was no stopping in the bumper-to-bumper line of traffic. So, pretending that he had trouble with his engine, Rohde's driver got out and pushed the jeep to the side of the road.

As the rest of the US vehicles ground past, their drivers' eyes intent on the road ahead which led to safety, he flung open the hood and pretended to be working on the motor, while the others, covered by the hood, wrenched the blackout covers from the headlights.

The team had just slammed the hood down again when, as Rohde related afterwards, 'A jeep rolled to a stop behind us. A captain raised his long legs over the side of the jeep and came towards us. In a deep voice he asked if he should tow us to the next motor transport outfit.' The driver scrambled into his seat, turned the key and the jeep's motor burst into life. Rohde thanked the captain and hurried back to his own jeep where the driver gunned the engine as if his life depended upon it, which perhaps it did. One minute later they had forced their way back into the column and were rolling westwards again. But Rohde wondered how the other teams were getting on. Would they notice in time that they were the only jeeps with blacked-out headlights?

One jeep team, under the command of Fritz Bussinger, had

already reached its objective, the bridge which spanned the River Meuse at Huy. Slowly the jeep trundled down the long steep incline to the bridge. Bussinger ordered the driver to take the vehicle into one of the side streets, while he went on on foot. Ignoring the handful of frozen sentries guarding the bridge, he marched across it and into the town on the other side, checking for wires and detonation charges. Officers passed him and Bussinger saluted them carefully. He didn't want to be stopped because he hadn't saluted.

In all Bussinger spent three hours in the area, noting everything of importance. For it was here that the advance guard of the 1st SS Division would cross, heading on from Huy to the coast and victory. Finally he started to walk back to the parked jeep. Just as he reached it, an American convoy with armoured cars and tanks rolled towards him and an officer in the first vehicle asked, 'Which way to Marchin?'

Bussinger reacted promptly. He pointed north, the opposite direction to Marchin, and explained that the Germans had captured several of the roads leading to the village. It would be better if the convoy made a wide detour to reach Marchin safely. The US officer thanked Bussinger and the convoy set off once more – *in the wrong direction*.

That was only one of a series of incidents in which the *Stielaugruppe* misled the retreating Americans and the reinforcements hurrying up to bolster the sagging front. One of Skorzeny's commando units, led by Sergeant Wilhelm Giel, set up a road block and, disguised as American MPs, started directing US traffic. When the advance party of the US 84th Infantry Division turned up. Giel directed them down the wrong road. Later Giel heard in a US radio broadcast that they had been missing for three days. Then Giel changed all the unit signposts, cut the communication wires strung along the trees lining the road and vanished.

An ammunition dump and a large POL (petrol, oil, lubricants) dump were discovered by another of Skorzeny's teams and destroyed. The markings of a minefield outside Eupen, which was the headquarters of the US V Corps, which was trying desperately to hold the shoulder of the breakthrough, were removed and American troops started being killed by their own mines.

Another leader of a *Stielau* team decided to scout the area

1. The cuff title of the Brandenburg Battalion.

2. "At the bridge at Gennep the team went into action well before dawn" (p.19).

3. "The mysterious Admiral Canaris, known behind his back as 'Father Christmas', due to his shock of snowy-white hair" (p.7).

4. Heinrich Himmler out shooting. He was apparently unconcerned by the fact that Hitler despised all blood sports.

5 + 6. The Brandenburgers in action in Russia in 1942.

7. "When he was sober Heydrich [*centre*] was cool, cruel and calculating" (p.27).

8. "Heydrich was assassinated by Czech parachutists flown from Britain" (p.46). Seen here is the Mercedes in which he was travelling when he was killed.

9. Hitler giving the address at Heydrich's funeral on 9 June, 1942.

10. Hitler and Franco at Hendaye, 24 October, 1940. "Later an exhausted Hitler said that he'd 'rather have four teeth pulled out than face another confrontation with the Caudillo'"(p.30).

11. The Brandenburgers prepare for their first attempt at long-range penetration by air: Egypt, March, 1941 (see p.32).

12. "Ritter [*left*] had been running agents into Britain since 1938" (p.30).

13. "[Eppler] spent much of his time in Cairo's night clubs, at the racecourse or with ladies of easy virtue" (p.47).

14. "Count Almaszy was going to guide the Brandenburgers through the trackless desert" (p.47).

15. "The door flew open and Captain 'Sammy' Sansom... stood there, pistol in hand" (p.54).

16. Happier times: Eppler, his daughter, his wife, Mrs Sansom, Captain Sansom in Cairo.

17. "The SS Captain was certainly worth looking at" (p.66). Otto Skorzeny in 1943.

18. Mussolini is greeted by Hitler in Berlin after his rescue in 1943 (see p.74).

19. The last survivor: a Tiger tank of Jochen Peiper's Battle Group of the 1st SS Panzer Division still at La Gleize, Belgium (see p. 117).

20. "Now every crossroad and bridge... was guarded by hurriedly assembled teams of American, French and Belgian soldiers" (p. 123). The great flap — December, 1944.

21. "Eighteen of the *Stielau* teams were shot as spies by the Americans" (p.127).

22. A happy bunch of Skorzeny's commanders in US uniform. They were not shot.

23. The leader of one of the teams which tried to guide Scherhorn's men out of Russia (see p.141).

24. "The mysterious General Gehlen [*left*], head of 'Foreign Armies East'"(p.139).

25. The Ardennes, Winter, 1944.

26 + 27. Skorzeny's commandos; *above*, going into action; *below*, training in winter uniforms.

28. The Alpine Redoubt. "[Gehlen] started removing his top secret
files and transferring them to hiding places in the German Alps" (p. 139).

29. "'The Americans,' he said, 'have seized the railway bridge across the Rhine at Remagen'"(p.147).

30. "'Now it's up to you frogmen to blow it up'" (p.147).

31. "Within minutes of reaching their objective the whole group had been shot, captured or drowned" (p.147) Two of the luckier ones being interrogated.

32. Skorzeny in his cell at Dachau, Summer, 1945.

around the Belgian frontier town of Malmédy. He rolled down the long hill which led into the town and saw to his horror that it was occupied by American engineers. So he decided to do some more reconnaissance and went directly to the centre of the town. He noted that the place was lightly defended and that the infantry in the barracks just outside were decidedly shaky. They were all reinforcements and he reckoned they wouldn't fight. Not once was he stopped or questioned by the engineers defending the place, which was fortunate, for he only spoke broken English. A few hours later he returned to Skorzeny's HQ at the Hotel du Moulin in the little hamlet of Engelsdorf* (very inaptly named, for 'the village of angels' was now occupied by some of the worst thugs in the German Army) and reported what he had seen to his chief.

It was encouraging news, yet Skorzeny couldn't make much use of it. The decisive breakthrough hadn't been made by the 1st SS Panzer Division yet. Peiper, at the head of his command group, was still trying to work his way out of the hills to the west of Engelsdorf, so Skorzeny couldn't yet use his 150 Panzerbrigade, disguised as Americans. It was all very frustrating because it seemed to Skorzeny that the time was ripe for a swift drive to the Meuse and beyond. So he waited impatiently at the Hotel du Moulin, drinking the bourbon left behind by General Anderson, the US Commander, when he had fled at the approach of the Germans.

Late that same dark afternoon Skorzeny's HQ started to receive radio signals from one of the teams which had actually set up camp on the eastern bank of the River Meuse outside Huy. It was the Rohde team. The men reported that they had got right up to the 19th-century stone bridge spanning the river. By the lights of vehicles crossing it in a steady stream, they could see it was guarded. 'There were a number of typical American tents on the eastern bank,' Rohde recalled, 'from which soldiers came and went all the time. Obviously they belonged to a guard company responsible for the bridge. Now we could see, too, the Americans positioning a searchlight on the other side of the river. Had they got wind of our mission?'

All this they radioed back to HQ, making the point that the vital bridge was only guarded by a company armed with hand

* Today Ligneuville.

119

weapons and with no flak or anti-tank guns in place. They begged to be allowed to come back; their luck wouldn't hold out for ever. Permission was granted and they were ordered to report to the headquarters of the Sixth SS Panzer Army as soon as possible with their vital information.

But, while Skorzeny fumed over the fact that he could take a bridge like that as easy as snapping his fingers, Peiper was virtually bogged down. There would be no decisive breakthrough for the 150 Panzerbrigade now. All the same Skorzeny's commandos were about to achieve one of the greatest German successes of the Battle of the Bulge.

Eight: The SS Kommandos 1944

'Es geht um Ganze.'*
FM Rundstedt to his troops,

16 December, 1944

* It's the whole hog.

Now tension was in the air. Once more refugees were streaming back from the border areas. In Belgium pictures of Churchill and Roosevelt, were swiftly removed from the windows. Civilians who had had dealings with Allied soldiers in the rear areas were shunned. Even the 'good-time girls' who worked behind Liège's main station or the Rue Neuve in Brussels were no longer so keen to sell their bodies to Allied troops. The Germans were coming back and the civilians did not want to be known as pro-Allied. There were all too many informers in Belgium and Luxembourg only too eager to denounce their fellow citizens to the Gestapo.

Now every crossroad and bridge in the rear areas was guarded by hurriedly assembled teams of Americans, French and Belgian soldiers. Montgomery was rushing up the leading elements of his 30 Corps and already one of those units, the 29th Armoured Brigade, was attempting to guard all the bridges south of Liége which spanned the Meuse.

With fifty-six German columns loose in the Ardennes, it was understandable that the defenders of these bridges, waiting in the freezing snow, were highly nervous. It was no different at the bridge in the small Belgian town of Aywaillé. It was guarded by a mixed force of US military policemen and hurriedly armed black service troops. According to one report by British Brigadier H. Essame of the 43rd Infantry Division, one had to be particularly wary of these coloured troops 'because they had already shot one American and two Belgians'.

In the segregated US army of those days, when both Eisenhower and Patton still talked typically of their 'darkies' and 'nigras', such behaviour was expected of blacks. Now, however, the black troops guarding the bridge at Aywaillé were going to play a role of great significance in the 'Big Flap' which was soon to develop.

About noon on Sunday, 17 December, a jeep was spotted approaching the roadblock. It contained three men in American uniform. Dutifully it began to slow down as the guards raised their weapons. The jeep driver braked. There was a small exchange in English. Then one of the MPs asked for the password. The driver paled and stuttered something.

'The password, buddy!' the MP said threateningly, as the black troops stared at the jeep's occupants with sudden interest. The jeep driver blustered something about not having been given a password. That was enough for the MP. Each soldier in the Liège area who was travelling that day *had* been given a password. He indicated, with a jerk of his tommy gun, that the three men in the jeep should get out.

Swiftly their identitites were established. They were PFC Charles W. Lawrence, PFC George Senzenbach and PFC Clarence van de Werth. Nothing very special about that. But while their identities were being checked, the blacks started to search the jeep. They struck gold almost immediately. These were not ordinary GIs, that was certain. In the rear, hidden under the seat, they discovered a huge roll of hundred dollar bills, as fresh as the day they had come off the printing press, which wasn't surprising. They had been printed the week before at a secret concentration camp printing plant, manned by convicted expert forgers.

For a while the searchers suspected they had captured three deserters, or perhaps black marketeers, for although their English was good, it wasn't perfect. But soon the blacks dug up, in the interior of the jeep, two British sten guns, two Colts, two German Walther pistols, plastic explosive and, most incriminatingly of all, a radio transmitter. Shortly afterwards they discovered the zippo lighters containing the L-pills.

Now the smallest of the three started to sing. His name was not George Senzenbach, but Wilhelm Schmidt and he was a corporal in the German Army. It was the sensation of that freezing Sunday. The soldiers crowded around him as he explained how he and the other two had set off from the neighbourhood of Monschau in Germany on the twelfth. Some days later, he related, they had successfully penetrated the US lines, posing as members of the US 5th Armored Division. Their mission had been 'infiltrating through the Americans and reporting the condition of the Meuse bridges and of the roads leading to those bridges'.

The NCO in charge waited to hear no more. He raced for his field telephone. In a matter of minutes he and his superior were in contact with headquarters in Liège. Headquarters were shocked. The Germans this far already (Aywaillé is just south of Liège)! Within thirty minutes a fleet of jeeps containing heavily armed MPs and members of the US field intelligence, the CIC, was on its way to Aywaillé. The top brass wanted to know all they could from the three prisoners, who would never see their homeland again. They would be dead before December was over.

It is not known what methods the CIC used on the three Germans to make them talk so fast. American intelligence agents were not too squeamish at the best of times. After all, back home in peacetime the 'third degree' had been standard operating procedure and higher headquarters were screaming out for information. So they made the German talk, and what a tale they had to tell!

Schmidt, who had been one of the first volunteers to join Skorzeny, told his interrogators, 'Early in November I reported to an SS camp at Friedenthal, where I was examined as to my linguistic ability by a board consisting of an SS, a *Luftwaffe* and a naval officer. I passed the test, but was ordered to refresh my English. For this purpose I spent three weeks at prisoner-of war camps in Kuestrin and Limburg, where large number of American troops were being held.'

Later, Schmidt said that he was posted to Grafenwoehr, where he was placed in a special unit. Here, 'our training consisted of studying the organization of the American army, identification of American insignia, American drill and linguistic exercises.' Now Schmidt had his interrogators on the edge of their seats. For he told them that he and his group had had the task of 'destroying headquarters and headquarters personnel'.

'What headquarters and what headquarters personnel?' the CIC demanded.

Now all those wild rumours which had circulated at Grafenwoehr the month before came out: the dash across France to relieve Lorient, the surprise attack on Montgomery's headquarters in Holland, the column of 'captured' Tiger tanks to meet up with the assassins assembling at the Cafe de la Paix.

'To do what?' the CIC agents asked.

'To kill General Eisenhower.'

It was all coming together. Skorzeny, the man who had rescued the Duce in 1943 the man who had tried to kill Tito a year later, who had kidnapped the son of the Hungarian dictator. Now he and his killers were gunning for the Supreme Commander. Ike had to be warned at once.

Now there were sightings of 'Skorzeny's killers', real or imagined, everywhere. At Dinant on the Meuse a scratch force under the command of a British Colonel named Brown had been set up as a last ditch force. At any minute they expected the arrival of the 2nd German Panzer Division.

Colonel Brown had reckoned that the Germans would approach the town from the south and there he had thrown a thin screen of men across the road. Behind them, where the road ran through an opening in the solid rock, his American engineers had thrown a necklace of Hawkins grenades across the road – a daisy chain, as it was known. In front of the grenades they had set up an strongpoint. Brown thought that if the Germans charged through the first two positions at speed they'd go right over the mine-grenades.

Suddenly an American jeep containing four men hurtled out of the darkness. Someone shouted at it to halt, but it kept on at speed while men waited for the disaster to come. As the jeep blew up and fell to the ground in a sheet of flame the engineers darted forward and tugged at the smouldering uniforms of the apparently dead GIs. But as the first man's combat jacket was tugged off the engineers were horrified to find beneath it the silver runes of the SS. Another of the Stielau teams had been discovered.

Next morning, half a mile away, Alf Miles and his pals in the 29th Armoured Brigade stopped another 'American' jeep. When the driver got out, he shook each British soldier's hand, mumbling something in a kind of fractured English. Alf asked, 'Can't you speak English?' His answer was, 'Yes, American English.' The man was arrested on the spot, yet another of Skorzeny's commandos.

On the same day, thirty miles away at Poteau near St Vith, the troopers of the 7th Armored Division stopped some suspicious-looking Americans riding three self-propelling guns of the 14th Cavalry, which had been virtually broken in the first two days of the great German offensive. 'Who are you?' the men of the 7th asked.

'We're E Company,' one of the Americans replied in stilted English. That was enough for the 7th Armored men. In the cavalry you didn't belong to a 'company' you belonged to a 'troop'. The men of the 7th opened fire immediately, mowing the men down mercilessly, more of Skorzeny's unfortunate pseudo-Americans.

Eighteen of the *Stielau* teams were shot as spies by the Americans. Three teams returned intact, having all reached their objectives on the Meuse, and three returned with one or more of their members killed or wounded by alert American sentries. But, despite their losses and the fact that no use could be made of their observations on the Meuse, the whole operation was a tremendous success. In the terms of what today would be called 'psychological warfare' it could be categorized as a major victory. Fewer than two hundred Germans had created confusion and alarm throughout the Allied camp, not only in Belgium and Luxembourg, but in France and even in Britain.*

At Versailles Colonel Gordon Sheen, Eisenhower's Chief of Counter-Intelligence, decided that Corporal Schmidt's story could not be ignored. He ordered that Eisenhower should be given immediate protection and removed from his private quarters at the Petit Trianon. Up until August this had been Field Marshal von Rundstedt's billet and it was thought the 'Skorzeny killers' would know every inch of the place. So Colonel Baldwin B. Smith, who was regarded as a perfect double for Eisenhower, was promoted to five star general and took Ike's place. If the killers were looking for a target it would have to be Smith.

From 20 to 26 December, with a desperate battle involving some three million men raging at the front, Eisenhower was a prisoner in his own quarters, cut off from the front and the decision-making processes. As his secretary-cum-mistress Kay Summersby noted: 'Security officers immediately turned head-quarters compound into a virtual fortress. Barbed wire appeared.

* See C. Whiting: *The March on London* for further details.

127

Several tanks moved in. The normal guard was doubled, trebled, quadrupled. The pass system bacame a matter of life and death instead of the old formality. The sound of a car exhaust was enough to halt work in every office, to start a flurry of calls to our office to inquire whether the boss was all right. The atmosphere was worse than that of a combat headquarters up at the front, where everyone knows how to take such a situation in their stride.'

General Strong, Eisenhower's Scottish Chief of Intelligence, protested that Sheen was going too far, but he was overruled. Eisenhower would have to obey orders.

The constant attention of a whole battalion of MPs angered Eisenhower so much that he once walked out of his office muttering to Kay Summersby, 'Hell's fire, I'm going for a walk. If anyone wants to shoot me, he can go right ahead. I've got to get out.'

Summersby wrote in her diary. 'I lay awake for hours envisioning death and worse at the hands of SS agents. Sleep seemed impossible with the tramp-tramp of heavy boots patrolling our roof.'

Captain Harry Butcher, Eisenhower's PR man, went to visit his boss and told him that he had been stopped by roadblocks everywhere on his way back from the front. He found Eisenhower thoroughly irritated by all the restrictions. 'There are all sorts of guards,' Eisenhower snorted, 'some with machine guns, around the house'. Butcher concluded that Eisenhower 'seemed pleased to have someone to talk with like me from the outside world.'

Butcher joked, 'Now you know how it must feel to be President and always under the watchful eye of the Secret Service.'

One wonders if, eight years later, when Eisenhower was elected the President of the United States, he remembered that quip and under what circumstances it was made.

The great scare spread from Supreme Allied Headquarters to Paris itself. A curfew was imposed. The capital was put out of bounds to all US Servicemen not on duty. The leave men vanished, to be replaced by grim-faced MPs looking for the 'Skorzeny killers'.

Naturally the 'damned Café de la Paix', as Skorzeny came to call it, was under special watch. There the CIC set up a permanent ambush, complete with field guns and tanks, lying in wait for the killers to rendezvous, presumably with Skorzeny at their head.

US General Hughes, one of Eisenhower's cronies, was twice refused entrance to his hotel because the sentries there didn't recognize him. That evening, in a rage, he stomped off to the Folies Bergères with his current girlfriend and found he'd broken the eight o'clock curfew for all US troops.

Spies, saboteurs and killers were spotted everywhere, even as far south as the Riviera. Hundreds of innocent American soldiers were arrested because the sentries didn't like the look of them or because they couldn't answer the questions the sentries put to them.

Field Marshal Montgomery had the tyres of his Rolls Royce shot out by US guards. Thereupon he demanded an American identification card from Eisenhower so that he wouldn't waste any more time trying to name the husband of Betty Grable to inquiring sentries. General Bradley, commander of the US 12th Army Group, removed the stars from his helmet and now used the back door of his HQ at Luxembourg's Hotel Alpha. Every night he slept in a different bedroom in case the killers came.

General Bruce Clarke, the defender of St Vith, now locked in a desperate battle with the Germans, was arrested by his own MPs. They wouldn't believe that he was an American general. Watching him, one of his men decided not to interfere because the only password he knew was 'Mickey Mouse' and he was sure that was out of date; he might get arrested too. Over and over again the General repeated, 'But I'm General Bruce Clarke of Combat Command B.'

'Like hell,' the MPs scoffed. 'You're one of Skorzeny's men. We were told to watch out for a Kraut posing as a one star general!

In the end the MPs released the irate general, but as General Bradley summed it all up after the war 'Half a million GIs were forced to play cat and mouse with each other each time they went on the road.'

It *was* a German victory.

But Skorzeny knew nothing of this. He was still bogged down at Engelsdorf on the heights above Malmédy because Peiper was making little progress in that vital drive for the Meuse. So it came as a kind of relief when, on 20 December, he contacted 6th SS Panzer Army's HQ at nearby Meyrode and asked for a mission, which was granted. He was to attack Malmédy with the three battle groups of his Brigade. This delighted Skorzeny, for, as we have seen, his men had reconnoitred the city and found it lightly defended. Not only that, but the US 9th Air Force had bombed Malmédy three times and inflicted hundreds of casualties on both civilians and troops. The US soldiers there were now calling the Ninth Air Force 'the American *Luftwaffe*'.

Although this was a conventional military operation, Skorzeny was not going to waste all the training in unconventional warfare that he had lavished on his Brigade. If it were possible, his camouflaged Panthers and handful of captured Shermans might lead the way for a surprise attack by the whole Brigade.

Lieutenant-Commander von Beer, an elderly naval officer, now disguised as a somewhat unlikely US lieutenant, was the first jeep commander to enter Malmédy. However, as he said to Skorzeny, 'I crossed the front line by mistake. It wouldn't have happened to me at sea, believe you me, *Obersturmbannführer*.'

He had ridden around the badly bombed town, the ruins still smoking from the third US attack, and found it virtually empty of Americans. He had been stopped, but by Belgian civilians, who asked him fearfully, 'Are the Germans coming back?' Von Beer answered truthfully that he didn't know and then fled back up the hill to Engelsdorf. Later he remarked, 'We got away with it that time because we had more luck than sense.'

But the elderly naval officer was not the only Skorzeny commando who had penetrated the Malmédy area before the Brigade attacked. On the same day Sergeant Keogan of the US 291st Engineers, which would bear the brunt of the defence, was working on detached duty on the road that led out of Malmédy up the heights towards Eupen. There he came across a massive traffic jam, with angry MPs trying to sort out the mess. A whole US regiment, the 16th of the famous US 1st Infantry Division, was snarled up bumper to bumper.

One of the MPs told Keogan, 'We had some boys going down to where the breakthrough is and some damned joker changed the road signs. They sent the whole outfit down the wrong road. When we got on the trail of it, there was two still standing out on the road turning 'em wrong.'

Sergeant Keogan asked who had changed the road signs. 'Krauts,' the MP said. 'In American uniform too. They had a jeep and when we got here they jumped in and made off so fast one of 'em was still standing on the front bumper hanging on to wire clippers. They hauled out of here going fifty miles an hour.'

Keogan decided he'd better be getting back to Malmédy. With Germans dressed in American uniforms loose everywhere, it would be safer back with the outfit.

Keogan's news increased the apprehension of an already jumpy garrison. The engineers had thought Malmédy a decent billet at first. Now they felt an attitude of hostility to them on the part of the civilians. They felt, too, that the locals were spying on them, ready to betray them to the Germans at the drop of a hat.

It was with a sigh of relief that Colonel Pergrim, the CO of the 291st Engineers, welcomed the arrival of some infantry from the 30th Infantry Division and a Norwegian service battalion, usually employed in cutting timber for the front.

Despite the reinforcements the men were jumpy. They all knew about the Malmédy massacre, the shooting of nearly 100 unarmed American prisoners by the SS, which had taken place on 17 December a mile away from the town. The Germans, so they had been told, weren't taking prisoners and that night it took a brave man to move from one position to the other. They were shooting first and asking questions afterwards. Some time after dark the Americans shot two of their own men dead thinking they were Germans.

On the 20th one of Skorzeny's commandos was captured in US uniform. He told his interrogators of the 30th Division, who didn't treat him particularly gently, that on the morrow Skorzeny would attack. A whole SS Panzer corps would attempt to break through to Peiper. Skorzeny's objective would be Malmédy itself.

The three colonels now commanding in Malmédy were alerted. They set off to put their defences in order. By noon on the morning of Thursday, 21 December, the mixed force of engineers, lumberjacks and infantry were ready and waiting. The question now was how and where would Skorzeny come?

Lieutenant Peter Mandt, now disguised as a corporal in the US Army, moved into his jump-off position with other tanks of the Brigade just after midnight. His Panther was disguised to look a bit like an American tank. Mandt was not really worried if it were not taken for the real thing. Before volunteering for Skorzeny's Brigade he had spent several years in combat in Russia. 'We knew we were going to lose the war,' he said afterwards, 'and regarded battle as some kind of gigantic lottery with the big prize – *survival!*'

Now Mandt's Panther rolled into position on the Falize road where it would be part of the left prong of Skorzeny's attack. The right prong would go in through Baugnez where, under the snow, lay the frozen bodies of the victims of the Malmédy massacre.

Mandt's Panther halted 100 yards from the railway station at the Malmédy viaduct, still undetected by the handful of Americans holding the town. To pass the time Mandt ordered his radioman to turn to the soldiers' favourite propaganda station, *Soldatensender Calais*, the propaganda station run by ex-*Daily Express* journalist Sefton Delmer.

However, this December night *Soldatensender Calais* was not as amusing as usual. Suddenly the music stopped and a harsh voice barked out, 'Take aim, fire!' This was followed by the sound of gunfire '*Mit diesen Salven,* 'the announcer said, '*endete ein weiteres Einsatzkommando Skorzeny's* (with these volleys another one of Skorzeny's commando teams met its end). The three Skorzeny commandos apprehended at Ambleve had been shot dead twenty miles away at Henri-Chapelle near Eupen.

The radioman switched off the radio. The men together in the chill gloom of the Panther were fatalists all right, but they wanted to give themselves a chance. They were going to be shot out of hand as spies if they were caught in American uniform. They started to strip off their GI uniforms and don paratroopers' overalls.

At 3.30 am, just as the prisoner had predicted, the attack began. From two directions the tanks came in, protected by infantry on both flanks, but almost immediately they ran into trouble. The engineers had strung trip wires across the open fields. To these wires they had attached flares. Now Skorzeny's infantry stumbled right into them, the flares exploded above their heads in a burst of icy-white flame.

Close to the Falize road Mandt and his crew got rid of the

Panther's 'American' camouflage and rattled into the attack. 'Night seemed turned into day,' he said later, 'Christmas trees* were coming down on all sides and already the American anti-tank cannon were firing. Armour piercing shells were hurtling towards us like glowing golf balls.'

T/5 Vincent Consiglio, Privates Mitchell and Spires of the 291 Engineers saw the lead tanks hurrying down the road towards them and knew they couldn't do much with only their rifles. They retreated until they came to a stone house held by a platoon of the 823rd Tank Destroyer Battalion. There they were assigned to lookout duties. Consiglio was put in the basement where he broke the little window and peered out into the glowing darkness. Only yards away was a tank decorated with the white star of the Allied forces, but it was German all the same. Next moment the Panther fired. Consiglio staggered upstairs. All the anti-tank men had been killed outright. The tank rumbled on.

The commandos made one last attempt to storm the railway embankment which ran west of the city. Consiglio, who had managed to rejoin the handful of defenders, volunteered to go back for more ammunition. He was told, 'You're a dead duck the minute you stick your nose out of this house.' Still he went. 'I never ran so fast in all my life. I really had wings on my feet,' he recalled after the war. 'You never know how fast you can go until you've got bullets nipping at your heels.'

He made it, only to run into trouble from his own side.

'Halt!' someone shouted.

Consiglio shouted the first word that came into his head: '*Kamerad!*'

Things turned nasty after that. The Americans defenders, manning a machine gun, thought they had captured one of Skorzeny's commandos. Consiglio was slapped around, badly kicked and then shoved against the nearest wall. His fellow Americans were going to shoot him! He was saved at the last moment by a US captain, who sent him back for reinforcements. But when he reached headquarters, it was in total confusion. The officers there thought that Skorzeny's commandos had broken through and were freely roaming around Malmédy. In fact, the attack on the left wing had failed miserably with 15 percent German casualties. Now it was up to Skorzeny's right wing.

---

* German soldiers' slang for multiple flares.

Nine: Skorzeny's Last Attack
1944

*Marschieren oder Krepieren**

Old German Army Saying.

* March or croak.

The commandos that Skorzeny had gathered at Engelsdorf for the attack on the right wing were a rough, tough and motley bunch. Some had complete sets of GI uniform, some were dressed as Germans, some wore a mixture of German and American clothing. It was the same with their vehicles – some German, some American, some hybrid, as well as British bren gun carriers and Humber scout cars. What would British vehicles be doing in the Ardennes so far from the British 21st Army Group? Still the men were tough, experienced and well-armed with automatics and plenty of grenades.

The brigade commander, who should have commanded the right wing thrust, had just been killed. So Skorzeny took over personally, though Hitler had expressly forbidden this. As his deputy, he took his old comrade, the blond-haired von Foelkersam. Skorzeny's attack was doomed from the start. As we have seen, the Americans had been reinforced and they were going to use a secret weapon – shells using the new proximity fuse invented by the British. The Pozit shell didn't need to hit the target. Proximity alone exploded it, making it a much more effective weapon than the ordinary shell.

Skorzeny's tanks hit the American tree-cutting battalion first – the 'Norwegians', as the Germans insisted on calling them. The 'Norwegians' stopped them dead, and over a hundred commandos were killed in the first five minutes of the attack.

Skorzeny, leading the main body down the Stavelot-Malmédy road, made better progress. They hit K Company of the 120th Infantry and the American infantrymen started to pull back. Skorzeny pushed on harder.

Lieutenant Nelson, in charge of K Company, rallied his men and they began to fight back. A sniper in US uniform crept close to the US positions and killed Nelson with one shot. Again it looked as if the company might bug out. Sergeant van der Kamp took charge and again the company rallied, but now it was officially ordered to withdraw. The situation looked grim for the defenders.

But now PFC Francis Currey took up the challenge. He holed up in a factory as the first German tank came into sight. Currey aimed his bazooka. The tank came to an abrupt halt, black smoke pouring from it. Currey shifted to a new position. He spotted three of the German commandos in a doorway. He raised his automatic rifle and pressed the trigger. All three fell. Time and again Skorzeny tried to get past this one man army – and failed!

Once again Currey changed position. He spotted five Americans pinned down by fire from three German tanks. Somewhere he found an armful of US anti-tank grenades and began slinging them at the stationary German tanks from the closest possible range. The German tankers abandoned their vehicles and the attack was over. Private First Class Francis Currey was to receive the Medal of Honor for his bravery. He had stopped the attack, but what he didn't know then was that he had just hammered the final nail into Skorzeny's coffin. The career of Germany's most celebrated commando leader was almost over.

That morning on the ridge overlooking Malmédy a disappointed Skorzeny watched as the first men of his Brigade came back in disarray. Among them was von Foelkersam. They joked together as the baron explained how he had been shot in the rump, but Skorzeny could see the exhaustion and disappointment in the other man's face and that told him all he wanted to know. He ordered a general withdrawal.

A little while later Skorzeny returned to his HQ at Engelsdorf. But as he was about to enter the Hotel du Moulin the air was rent by the howl of a salvo of incoming shells. Skorzeny raced for cover, but he was too late. Blood started to gush from a wound in his face.

A little later he was operated on without benefit of anaesthetics because he wanted to keep a clear head. It was typical of him. He emerged with a thick bandage around the upper part of his face and a headache which would last for weeks, temporarily blind in one eye.

Six days later what was left of 150 Panzerbrigade was withdrawn over the German frontier, soon to be broken up. The surviving members of the *Jagdkommando* returned to their headquarters at Friedenthal. There von Foelkersam asked Skorzeny for a regular frontline assignment and Skorzeny agreed to let him go. He gave him the command of the Eastern Skorzeny Group. They were never to see each other again.

2

During the Battle of the Bulge Colonel General Heinz Guderian, Germany's leading tank expert had reported to the Führer that the Russians were going to take advantage of Germany's engagement in the West. Soon the Red Army would go over to the attack. He maintained that the Russians had a large number of rifle divisions, plus scores of tank divisions, waiting for the most opportune moment to assault the weakened German front in the East.

Hitler pooh-poohed Guderian's fears. The Eastern Front was quiet. The Russians were bluffing, he said scornfully. Oh yes, on paper they seemed to have a large number of rifle divisions, but their average rifle division contained only 7,000 men while its German equivalent had 12,000. As for the Russian armoured divisions, they 'didn't have a tank to their name'.

Working himself up into one of his artificial rages which had made many a battle-hardened general quail, he cried, 'It's the greatest imposture since Ghengis Khan! Who is responsible for producing all this rubbish?'

The officer responsible was the mysterious General Reinhard Gehlen, head of 'Foreign Armies East', the oddly named Intelligence Service of the Germany Army in Russia. For weeks his agents had been active behind the Red Army's lines, trying to establish what Stalin's intentions were now that the cream of the *Wehrmacht*, including most of its panzer division, were committed to the Battle of the Bulge. It had been Gehlen who had briefed Guderian for that disastrous Christmas Eve meeting with Hitler.

For Gehlen Guderian's lack of success had been the last straw. He realized that Hitler had closed his ears to anything he didn't want to hear. So he made some decisions about his own future. Secretly he started removing his top secret files and transferring them to hiding places in the German Alps. When Germany lost the war, those files would be invaluable to the Americans, he reasoned. They would ensure that he and his fellow intelligence officers would have a future, come what may.*

All the same the General continued to carry out his duties. Now, as December, 1944, gave way to January, 1945, he involved himself in a dozen desperate little schemes to delay the inevitable defeat, which he knew must come soon. With Schellenberg and Skorzeny, who was still recovering from his wound, he launched parateam after parateam behind Russian lines.

By the first week of January, while they prepared to launch their great offensive, the Russians had only occupied the main cities on their line of march. Behind them they had left great areas where the Germans and their Russian, Ukrainian and Polish collaborators could still operate with relative freedom. As Skorzeny recorded in his autobiography, many of the German telephone lines were still intact and operating weeks after the Russians had passed by. Indeed a German firm in Lodz in Poland had telephoned Berlin, when the Red Army had already crossed the border into the Reich, to ask if the firm should take up production again. The Russians had simply passed through the city without any attempt to set up any kind of administration. The reply of the Berlin head office is not known, but the Lodz anecdote was indicative of the confused situation behind the Russian lines.

Now, with the help of Skorzeny's *Jagdkommando*, which contained many Russian-speaking Germans and troopers from half-a-dozen Eastern European countries, Gehlen ordered numerous raids behind the Russian front. Some of these raids were aimed at sabotaging Russian communications. Others were spy missions. But the most important were those aimed at contacting and rescuing the large numbers of German soldiers who had been cut off by the Red Army's advance.

One such operation was given to Gehlen and Skorzeny by Jodl, Hitler's Chief of Operations, 'one which is especially important for the High Command to wash its hands of,' as Radl, Skorzeny's adjutant cynically, commented.

---

* They did. Within six months of the war ending Gehlen was in Washington. Soon his 'Gehlen Organization', as it was called, would become a mainstay of the new CIA in Europe.

During the summer débâcle in the East, some twenty-five German divisions had collapsed, leaving thousands of German soldiers behind the Russian lines. Some of the German units trapped had refused to surrender even when their divisional and corps commanders had ordered them to do so. One such unit, made up of two thousand men from a dozen different regiments, had been gathered together by a stubborn, hard-bitten officer, Lieutenant-Colonel Scherhorn.

For weeks the 'Scherhorn Group', as it was called, had been moving westward deep in the heart of Russia, which Skorzeny knew was still a long way from the nearest German positions. But they were becoming desperate. Their radio messages, according to Jodl, indicated that they were about at the end of their tether. Could he help?

Skorzeny had always had a soft spot for a brave man and, although Gehlen warned him that the radio messages from Scherhorn might be a trap, he flew back from Jodl's HQ determined to do what he could.

Two days later a very unlikely rescue team paraded before him at Friedenthal. There were about thirty of them. Their leaders were Baltic Germans who spoke Russian fluently. The rest were ethnic Russians, ex-POWs, deserters and the like who had been recruited into the *Jagdkommando* to work for their former enemies. But there was little difference now between the two ethnic groups. All had their hair shorn to the scalp in Red Army fashion.

None had shaved for the last forty-eight hours. Nor had they washed very much. They gave off that particular sour Russian odour, composed of sweat, garlic and the black coarse tobacco the Red Army smoked. Clad in earth-brown Russian smocks and carrying round-barrelled Russian tommy guns, they looked typical 'Ivans', as the German soldiers called their Red Army enemies. Skorzeny seemed pleased. At least they looked the part.

The first group, code-named 'A', took off in one of the four-engined long-range Condors provided by the special *Luftwaffe* squadron, KG 200, which always flew these clandestine missions. For five hours, flying at very high altitude, the Condor covered many hundreds of miles of Russian-held territory before dropping the team. Some hours later the first message was received at the *Jagdkommando's* HQ. It was short and not very encouraging:

141

'Poor landing. Enemy has spotted us. We're under machine-gun fire.' That was the last heard of Group A.

Undeterred, Skorzeny sent out Group B. For five nights nothing was heard from them and Skorzeny started to think that Gehlen might have been right after all. The whole operation was a Soviet trick. Then on the sixth day an excited deciphering clerk rushed into his office crying, '*Obersturmbannführer*, we've got them!' Group B had not only landed safely, but they had actually linked up with Colonel Scherhorn and his trapped men. Sixty minutes later Skorzeny was talking to the exhausted Colonel over the radio. He needed supplies, and he needed them badly.

Encouraged, Skorzeny flew out another team. It disappeared without trace. Group D followed. It landed safely and without incident. But it failed to find Scherhorn. What were they to do, hundreds of kilometres behind Russian lines? The NCO in charge, an SS Sergeant, decided to attempt the impossible and walk back with his men to the German lines. And the group succeeded. The sergeant even had the nerve to enter a Soviet officers' mess where he was toasted as a fellow officer. A few weeks later, after an epic march, he reached the German lines in Lithuania where he reported to Skorzeny by telephone: 'Reporting for duty, sir. No casualties.'

Now that Skorzeny had made contact, he set about arranging some sort of airlift to bring Scherhorn and his men out. But Scherhorn reported back that his men were too weak to clear runways in the snowbound forests in which they were hiding. So Skorzeny ordered a doctor to be parachuted in, but he broke both legs on landing. A second doctor was sent. He started to build up the trapped men's strength and tend their wounded. Work on the runway was begun and Skorzeny began sending in paradrops of food and supplies, but these attracted the unwelcome attention of the Red Air Force.

Skorzeny did some quick thinking. Two hundred miles from Minsk there was a series of frozen lakes. If Scherhorn could fight his way to the lakes, there would be no need to build a runway for the rescue planes to land on.

Scherhorn and his men set off in the midst of a blizzard. The next day the Colonel radioed that he had covered six miles. It wasn't much but at least he was moving. Mile after mile under terrible conditions, fighting not only snowstorms and blizzards, but Russians and even wolf packs.

142

As time passed Skorzeny's supply planes were cut. Desperately he fought to obtain more air transport but Gehlen washed his hands of the operation. By now he was convinced that the whole thing was a Russian trick. But Skorzeny persisted. Then, after fourteen weeks, he received a radio message from Scherhorn – if it was really him. His advance party had reached the lakes.

By this time Skorzeny was down to one plane a week. Now, with victory in sight, he was informed that there was no fuel even for the single supply plane. Berlin ordered that the flights must stop and that was that.

Colonel Scherhorn radioed. 'Where are the planes? Send to fetch us. Hurry. We are running out of food.'

There was nothing Skorzeny could do. As a last gesture, he ordered the award of the Knight's Cross of the Iron Cross to be dropped by the last plane to the SS Commando who had found the Scherhorn group. It was dropped successfully and it was acknowledged by Scherhorn, if it really was he. Perhaps that high award, with its blue and white ribbon holds pride of place on some Russian wall to this day.

Another of these joint Gehlen-Skorzeny missions behind the Russian lines was more successful. Under the command of Walter Girg, whom Skorzeny had originally wanted to turn down for the *Jagdkommando* because he was 'too pretty' and he lisped, a mixed group of Germans and ethnic Germans born in Rumania penetrated the Russian lines in the mountains between Russia and Rumania. Their orders were 'to block the Carpathian mountain passes, reconnoitre behind the enemy, wreck his communications and help German civilians to safety.'

It was a tall order for such a small group. But 23-year-old Lieutenant Girg was undismayed. He split his group into four and ordered each party to block a separate pass, which they did successfully for several days. Then they aided several hundred Rumanian Germans – 'the Seven Mountain Saxons' as they were called – who had been established in that country for generations to escape from the advancing Red Army.

A few days later Girg's luck ran out. After passing through the town of Kronstadt, newly captured by the Red Army, disguised as soldiers of the Rumanian Army, which was now fighting on the Russian side, Girg and four of his men ran into a Russian ambush.

A fierce fire fight broke out, but when the Germans' ammunition ran out they were forced to surrender. Naturally the Red Army men took them for spies, which they were. They were stripped of their uniforms and two of the ethnic Germans were beaten to death by the Russians. Girg and the other two were told they were going to be shot. Girg realized that this was his last chance. He took a deep breath. Then he was up and running as fast as his feet would carry him. The Russians gave chase but Girg eluded them and finally fell, completely exhausted into a swamp. More dead than alive, he staggered through the freezing night in the general direction of the German lines. Luck was on his side once more. Some time later he reached a German outpost near the small town of Morosvasacheli. He was safe.

While the desperate SS commandos continued to fight and die in the East, still believing in the *Endsieg* – the final victory – which Hitler had promised them, realists like Gehlen and Skorzeny planned for the defeat. In essence they believed that they could still fight Germany's cause even though Germany would now undoubtedly lose the war. Soon the Western Allies would have to confront their erstwhile ally, Russia. So they swallowed the new concept being ingeniously created by the Minister of Propaganda and Public Enlightenment, Dr Josef Goebbels. It went something like this. Germany had been the aggressor and had committed horrendous war crimes over the last five years. But it had done so to create a 'New Europe', firm in its determination to fight the 'communist beast' from the East.

But how to secure Germany's power in defeat? The Goebbels-Skorzeny-Gehlen answer was to create a power base for the beaten nation's future, one based on money and secret knowledge. Hitler would have to go. The Germany of the future could no longer afford to be associated with the architect of the war of aggression and the holocaust. But the survivors need assets which would find them the favour of the soon to be victorious Americans and, in due course, would allow them also to resume their rightful place as Europe's premier power.*

Thus, while Gehlen was employing his energies and his agents

* It has taken post-war Germany fifty years to do this. But, as the author writes in 1995, it is clear that this is what has happened.

in transferring the invaluable intelligence he possessed on the Soviet state and its armed forces to the West to offer in due course to the Americans, Skorzeny was ensuring that huge amounts of gold and diamonds were sent to the same area of Bavaria and Austria to be hidden there until after the defeat.

Most of the top Nazis already had their families tucked safely away in what the Allies would come to know as the National Redoubt. Now the Gehlen intelligence files and the wealth shipped by Skorzeny followed.

Using methods he had perfected during his years in covert operations, Skorzeny transported millions to the area. Great quantities of gold taken from the mouths of those who had died in concentration camps were buried throughout Bavaria. Diamonds and rare *objets d'art* went too. Once he sent fifty kilograms of gold bars, fifty cases of gold coins, two million US dollars, two million Swiss francs, five cases containing diamonds and precious stones, plus a stamp collection reputedly worth five million gold marks.

Then, in the midst of all this, he was summoned to Hitler's HQ to carry out one last wartime mission.

Late on the morning of 7 March, 1945, Lieutenant Karl Timmermann's A Company of the US 9th Armored Division found itself on the heights just above the Rhenish town of Remagen. One mile away the Ludendorff Railway Bridge across the Rhine was still intact, with men and vehicles crossing it, bound eastwards, in a steady stream. In that first week of March it was the only bridge along the whole length of the German Rhine that was still standing. Shortly it was to be become, for a few days, 'the most famous bridge in the world'.

For a while Timmermann's superiors thought of shelling the bridge. Then General Hoge, the 9th Armored's assistant divisional commander, appeared. At first he berated the soldiers for being so slow in capturing Remagen. Then he said, 'You know it would be nice to get that bridge while we're at it.' The idea of capturing the railway bridge and altering the whole remaining course of the war in the West had been born.

By two o'clock that afternoon Timmermann, who had been born thirty miles away from Remagen and hadn't spoken English till he was three, was leading his company to the western end of the 1,000-foot-long bridge.

145

For a while they contented themselves with sniping at the tower-like structure at the other end, which at once alerted the German defenders to the fact that the Americans had arrived. So they detonated the first of the charges buried in and about the wrought-iron structure. Timmermann watched as the Germans scurried around, preparing to blow the remaining charges. Then he made his decision: 'We've got orders to cross,' he announced calmly.

Sergeant Sabia objected. 'It's a trap,' he blurted out. 'Once we get in the middle, they'll blow the bridge up.'

'Orders are orders,' Timmermann snapped. 'All right, let's go.'

There was no dramatic rush to capture the bridge. Unlike the virile heroes of the movie made about it a quarter of a century later, 'Timmermann's GIs thought the bridge looked like sudden death and were hesitant. Their stomachs were queasy too, for some of them had looted the cellars of the houses lining the riverbank and had drunk a lot of unaccustomed white wine. But they moved out all the same and as they did so a Major Deevers cried *after* them, "Come on, fellers. I'll see you on the other side and we'll all have a chicken dinner!"'

The infantrymen found the first explosive charge and snipped through the connecting wires. Almost immediately two machine guns opened up from the towers at the other end. The attack bogged down.

'Goddam, why let a couple of snipers hold up a whole battalion?' Sergeant de Lisio yelled. 'Let's get off this damn bridge. If it goes, we *all* go!' And with that he ran ahead, zig-zagging wildly, while the air around him sang with bullets. He rounded up five frightened Germans, crouching over a jammed machine gun. Then he ran inside one of the towers. He pelted up the stairs. A drunken officer and a soldier stood there. The officer staggered towards the detonating device in the corner. De Lisio fired a quick burst around the officer's feet. Both Germans then surrendered.

Meanwhile young Alex Drabik was searching for him. He cried, 'De Lisio must be over there – alone! Let's go!' A few moments later Alex Drabik became the first American to cross the German Rhine on active duty in the Second World War. Five minutes after that Karl Timmermann became the first US officer to do so. By nightfall a whole US division had started to pour

146

across. By dawn a whole US corps would be following. The Rhine had been crossed at last!

The next day Skorzeny was summoned to see the Führer. The latter congratulated him on his efforts in the East and then excused himself, adding 'Jodl will tell you why I summoned you to Berlin.'

Hitler left and Jodl placed a map on the table in front of Skorzeny. He pointed to the Rhine. 'The Americans,' he said, 'have seized the railway bridge across the Rhine at Remagen. The *Wehrmacht* failed to destroy it in time. Now it's up to your frogmen to blow it up. There is no time to lose. The Führer is depending upon you.'

Skorzeny left at once for Friedenthal where he briefed his 'Danube Frogman Group' (they had trained on that river, hence the name). He didn't try to gloss over the dangers. He knew the Americans would already have made defensive preparations to guard the vital bridge. 'The water's just about freezing,' he informed the frogmen. 'Now the Americans are well established on the east side of the Rhine and will be searching for you. I know they've already set up several searchlights in the area and will keep the bridge brightly lit at all times. I am asking for volunteers. I'm not *ordering* anyone to go.'

As one every man stepped forward.

Skorzeny smiled approvingly. 'We'll leave at midnight.'

The frogmen were in position six hours later. They drifted with the current between the high banks of the Rhine, carrying their explosives in watertight rubber bags. 'There were six of us,' Rudi Gunter, one of the group, recalled later. He wouldn't be going with the others but would remain with Skorzeny. 'But we had synchronized our watches with the frogmen and began our surprise attack exactly forty-five minutes later. By that time Skorzeny thought the frogmen would be in the vicinity of the bridge.'

Unknown to the six who were to carry out the attack, the frogmen who had survived the icy swim down the Rhine were trapped by the searchlights posted on both banks next to the bridge. Within minutes of reaching their objective the whole group had been shot, captured or drowned.

'We didn't know that,' Gunter remembered. 'So we made a sneak raid on the Americans on the east side of the bridge, trying to draw their attention. Just as Skorzeny gave the order for us to retreat to our jeeps before the Americans caught up with us, I was wounded in the leg. I couldn't walk. Skorzeny didn't say a word. He just reached down, picked me up and carried me to the nearest jeep. We only just got out of the area alive.'

The failed attack on the Remagen Bridge, which collapsed two days later, was Skorzeny's last commando raid of the Second World War. It marked the end of a remarkable career in covert operations, which far outshadowed those of such British commando and SAS leaders as 'Mad Mike' Calvert and David Stirling. Skorzeny had not just aimed at tactical military victories; he had tried to gain major political successes, engineered by force of arms. Soon Skorzeny would be on the run – indeed, in a way, he would be on the run for the rest of his life. But never again would there be anyone like this scarfaced Austrian giant who had helped to change the course of the Second World War.

Ten: Werewolves
1945

WERE-WOLF: a prehistoric WGmc
compound whose constituents are
represented by OE wer man and by OE
wulf-wolf: a person transformed into a wolf
or capable of assuming a wolf's form

Webster's New Collegiate Dictionary

The drone of the captured Flying Fortress which had brought them to this remote border area died away to the east. They had joined up without difficulty after the drop; the DZ had been picked well; no one had spotted them; they had come down totally unnoticed in this 'three country corner', as the locals called it.* Operation Carnival had got off to a good start.

But Lieutenant Wenzel, their mysterious leader who claimed he had once belonged to the Brandenburgers and that he had been with Skorzeny when the latter had rescued Mussolini two years earlier, gave them no time to congratulate themselves. He switched on the blue torch clipped to the pocket of his parachute overalls and ordered them to start unpacking what the youngest of the Werewolf team, 16-year-old ex-Hitler Youth member Morgenschweiss, called their 'food bomb'. They began to empty the two-metre-long aluminium container which held their supplies for the mission. Then they set off with Hennemann, a former border guard who knew the area intimately, in the lead.

There were six of them: Wenzel in his mid-20s; Hennemann and his pal, another ex-border guard, Heidorn, both in their thirties; the boy Morgenschweiss; Leitgeb, an SS man from Austria, and the woman. She was a former Hitler Maiden leader, fat-faced, sulky and looking older than her 24 years. Of all the group of potential murderers she was the most fanatical.

Then the strange little group, who had been training for this sort of mission all winter, set off to find their victim, marching through woods still filled with the rusting tanks and trucks of the

* The area around Aachen between Holland, Belgium and Germany.

151

previous September. Disparate as their backgrounds and motives were, they were linked by two things – they all knew the city in which their victims lived like the backs of their hands and they had come to kill!

After an hour or so they arrived at the border, a line of weathered granite stones. The two ex-border guards knew exactly where they were. In the thin blue light of Wenzel's torch, they buried the money they had been given at HQ under one of the stones. They had been told it was for 'an English agent'; more they didn't know. They pushed on.

Then they saw a couple coming down the path. 20-year old Josef Saive, a Dutch border guard, rifle slung carelessly over his shoulder, was walking with his girlfriend through the forest with his arm round her waist. It wasn't exactly regulations, but his boss, Sergeant Finders, was back at the tiny border post and was probably fast asleep in front of the stove. Now, as Saive saw the dark shapes, he knew instinctively that something was wrong. He slipped the rifle from his shoulder and whispered to his girl friend, 'Go back and tell Sergeant Finders to get help.' And she ran back the way she had come.

Saive stepped into the middle of the trail, ready for trouble. 'Jost was a keen boy,' Sergeant Finders recollected years later. 'He had visions of glory. He wanted action.' Now he levelled his rifle and cried, 'Hands up!'

Panic broke out among the six Werewolves. Surprisingly enough, it was the boy who acted first. In one swift movement he fired his pistol and flung himself down the bank to his right.*

Morgenschweiss's first shot hit Saive and he fell to the ground.

As Saive fell, the woman, whose name was Ilse Hirsch, rolled down the embankment to her left and started to run. As the first light of dawn coloured the sky she realized that she was near their objective.

On the skyline she could see the skyline of Aachen. For six months Germany's oldest and holiest cities had been occupied by the Americans. They were running it with the aid of their German puppets. But it was the chief puppet that she had come to deal with. Who he was she didn't know as yet, but she was determined to find out

---

* It was only many years later than Erich Morgenschweiss learned (from the author) that Saive was a miner's son like himself and that the Dutchman's native language was German like his.

152

It was now six o'clock on the morning of 22 March, 1945. On the Rhine, fifty miles away, the Allies were preparing for the great river crossing which would take place in the next 36 hours, watched by Churchill and Eisenhower. But deep to their rear, in territory which had been occupied since the autumn of the previous year, the first, and last, great Werewolf operation was under way.

The fall of the city of Aachen had angered Himmler. It was the first German city to fall to the Allies. It angered him even more that the local populace had not fled when ordered to do so but had stayed behind to await the American occupiers. In an enraged letter to General Gutenberger, the SS Police Chief for the West and part of the Werewolf Organization, he wrote: 'From the enemy press it is clear that in some areas occupied by the Anglo-Americans the local population is behaving in a manner without honour. I order that immediately in those areas which had been captured, the guilty parties should be brought to justice. Now we should attempt to *educate* the population in question by the execution of the death penalty *behind the front*.'

Gutenberger, who already knew that he was on the Allies' list of wanted war criminals, decided to let sleeping dogs lie; he didn't want to get any deeper into the mess than he was already. But a couple of weeks later, Pruetzmann, now head of the Werewolves, came to visit him in Düsseldorf. Just before he left he said to Gutenberger, 'And by the way what have you done about Aachen?'

Gutenberger had looked puzzled, 'Aachen?'

'Yes, that swine who the *Amis* have made burgomaster.'

'What about him?'

'You've got to liquidate him, haven't you,' Pruetzmann snapped.

'Yes,' Gutenberger had said, 'I know.' But he said the words without conviction.

Thus the idea of the murder of the unknown chief burgomaster of Aachen was born, 'Operation Carnival' as it was later known. Lieutenant-Colonel Neinhaus, an old crony of Gutenberger, took over the training of the new Werewolf organization in the Rhineland in the medieval castle at Hülchrath, some fifty miles from Aachen. Here he gave the Aachen assignment to the mysterious SS Lieutenant Wenzel, who maintained he had been born in South Africa, although he spoke only broken English, and who, according to his own account, had been involved in covert operations with the Brandenburgers from the beginning of the war.

As the training progressed, Wenzel picked his own team from the trainees, all of whom had lived or worked in the Aachen area, including the two former border guards Heidorn and Hennemann. They were less than enthusiastic for an operation which they regarded as *Himmel-fahrtskommando**, but they did know the frontier area well and they had operated for some time as *passeurs*, taking messages back and forth through enemy lines.

But while Wenzel picked and trained his team Gutenberger still hesitated. He was determined to survive the war somehow, even though the crimes he had committed in Poland would obviously hang over his head in the case of an Allied victory. Then in early December Himmler shocked Gutenberger into action with a message demanding: *'What has happened in the matter of the chief burgomaster of Aachen?'*

Fortunately for Gutenberger, his plan of action had to be shelved due to the start of the Battle of the Bulge. But by February, 1945, that battle had been won by the Allies and Himmler gave Gutenberger a direct order to carry out Operation Carnival. His message to the police chief read: 'The Chief Burgomaster of Aachen is sentenced to death. The sentence is to be carried out by [Werewolf].'

Gutenberger passed on the order to Lieutenant-Colonel Neinhaus, who trained the terrorists, who, in his turn, gave it to Wenzel. The operation was on. Two weeks later the murder squad flew off in the captured Flying Fortress, dropping a Belgian agent over Brussels (he was captured immediately) before landing in the region just south of Aachen. We know the rest.

Now, in the third week of March, with Ilse Hirsch lost somewhere or other, the five men were debating whether to give up. Wenzel and Morgenschweiss kept their own council. Leitgeb was for having a look round Aachen while the two border guards were for immediate surrender.

In the end they decided they'd wait a little longer. They'd send a group from their camp, deep in the heart of the Aachen Forest north of the city, to have a closer look at the situation. Leitgeb

* An Ascension Day mission, ie a one-way ticket to heaven.

154

and Morgenschweiss would do the recce while the rest guarded the camp.

It was Erich Morgenschweiss who first spotted Ilse Hirsch in the city. They were standing at the corner of the Auguststrasse watching the American trucks heading for the front and hungry civilians in search of food when he saw her. Hurriedly he crossed the street. 'Ilse,' he whispered. She turned round in fright. Then she recognized Morgenschweiss and relaxed. The young man jerked his head backwards and her eyes followed the direction. Standing against a shell-pocked wall was Leitgeb, one hand dug deeply into his pocket. He was holding the butt of his pistol just in case. If she had betrayed them, she wouldn't have lived long.

But Ilse had in fact shown more initiative than any of the male Werewolves. Not only had she found out who the Burgomaster of Aachen was – a former lawyer named Franz Oppenhoff – but she had also discovered that he lived at 252 Eupenerstrasse in the suburbs. She had even been inside the place and now knew its layout perfectly.

On the pretext of asking for a glass of water she had been admitted to the Burgomaster's house. To her surprise she found that the housemaid had a visitor, pretty, dark-haired, 16-year old Christel Schuetz. For a moment she had panicked. Christel had once been in her own group of Hitler's Maidens. But the girl had said nothing until she caught up with her after she had left the house. Christel had then invited her to spend the night at her own bombed-out house.

Now back at the forest camp, she gave the others a full briefing. Oppenhoff was a married man with three small children. The house had to be entered by the cellar door because the front door had been damaged in the month-long siege of Aachen and wouldn't open. Oppenhoff's closest neighbours were out of earshot. There were some Americans in the area, but they usually took no notice of the civilians unless they were out looking for 'frowlins'. On both sides of the houses were woods into which they could easily escape once they had carried out their mission.*

Squatting on his bed of branches, Wenzel listened intently to Ilse's excited monologue. When she was finished, he said, 'We're

---

* Frau Oppenhoff told the author that, due to fact that the Americans suspected an attempt might be made on her husband's life, no photographs of him were allowed to be taken. But a newsreel camera did get some footage of him, though the killers weren't aware of this.

155

going to do it.' He pointed to Leitgeb: 'You and me.' Then at Hennemann: 'You, too'.

It was Palm Sunday, 1945 and the last day of Franz Oppenhoff's life.

Oppenhoff was very tired. For six months he had been the American-appointed Burgomaster and he was sick of them. He was equally sick of the German civilians he ruled over; they were always moaning and complaining about the regulations, the food, the lack of fuel and so on. And he was afraid. As he had told his wife when she had returned to Aachen with the children in February, 'Somewhere out there is a paratrooper already assigned to assassinate me.'

This Palm Sunday weekend Oppenhoff and his wife worked on their vegetable patch together before putting the children to bed. Then, leaving them in the care of the 25-year old maid Elisabeth, they went over to the house of their neighbour Dr Faust where they had a couple of glasses of schnapps. At about ten o'clock they were interrupted by the excited voice of the maid calling, 'Herr Oppenhoff, Herr Oppenhoff, There are American soldiers here. They want to talk to you.'

The Burgomaster rose instantly. American soldiers! What did they want with him at this time of night? 'All right, Elisabeth,' he said. 'I'm coming.' Pulling on his official armband, he turned to Faust and said, 'You speak English. You'd better come with me.' And together they strode over to Oppenhoff's house. Wenzel was waiting for them.

'What do you want?' Faust asked in English.

Wenzel replied in German. Oppenhoff started back. Was this the paratrooper he had always feared?

'We're German airmen,' Wenzel lied. 'We were shot down near Brussels three days ago. Now we're trying to make out way back to the German lines. What about getting us passes, *Herr Burgomaster*?'

Oppenhoff shook his head. 'I can't do that. You should report to the Americans and give yourself up. The war's nearly over anyway. It's only a matter of days.'

Now Leitgeb stepped out of the shadows. The Austrian's greeting was hard and to the point. He said harshly, 'Heil Hitler!'

Faust started. It was a long time since he had heard those

156

words. Then he saw the butt of a pistol sticking out Leitgeb's pocket. Oppenhoff was just saying, 'Let me get you something to eat,' when Faust cut in with, 'I'll go back to the house and see what I can find out for you.' And before the two men had time to protest, he was off, walking quickly back to his own house.

Oppenhoff then turned to the flustered maid. 'They're German fliers, Elisabeth. Make them a couple of sandwiches, if you can find something.' And he followed her through the door into the darkness of the cellar.

Leitgeb hissed urgently, 'When he comes up again. Be quick. The other's gone off to warn the *Amis*.'

There was the sound of footsteps from below. It was Oppenhoff coming back with a plate of thick black bread sandwiches. The footsteps grew closer. The traitor came through the door, but Wenzel did not fire.

'*Do it!*' Leitgeb hissed, but still Wenzel hesitated.

'You coward,' Leitgeb spat and snatched Wenzel's pistol which was fitted with a long silencer. At that range he couldn't miss. His bullet hit the Burgomaster in his left temple.

Back at his own home Faust told the little circle about the Burgomaster's strange visitors. Irmgard Oppenhoff's eyes grew wide with fear. As she said later, 'the news went through me like an electric shock.'

She jumped to her feet. 'We can't leave my husband alone with them. For heaven's sake if they are Germans and my husband gives them anything to eat, it might cost him his life.' Turning to Dr Op de Hit, a friend of her husband who was also present, she said, 'Will you come with me?'

He rose to his feet. 'Yes, come on,' he answered.

Wenzel, still mesmerized by the sight of the dead Oppenhoff slumped on the cellar steps, heard them. 'There's somebody coming,' he whispered. 'Let's go.'

Leitgeb grabbed him. 'Wait a moment. We've got to have proof.' He bent and ripped off the official American armband.

Suddenly there was a ragged volley of shots from close by. The Americans had come to investigate why the wires had been cut. Now they had spotted the civilian out long after curfew time and were shooting at him. Hennemann started to run for the woods. Suddenly he became aware of someone running close behind him. He halted and drew his pistol. Then he saw his pursuer's face. It was Wenzel. 'Where's Sepp?' he asked, meaning Leitgeb.

'On the other side of the road,' Wenzel gasped, 'He's all right. Come on, let's get out of here quick.'

Hennemann needed no urging. Together they ran up the side of the road, doubled low, heading for the safety of the woods.

At the house Frau Oppenhoff's hand flew to her mouth as she saw her 42-year old husband crumpled on the steps. She stumbled back against Dr de Hit. '*Der Franz . . . der Franz ist tod.*'

The Doctor nodded. Franz Oppenhoff was dead.

Operation Carnival, that cynically code-named Werewolf mission (for this was the month of the German carnival in the Rhineland) was over.

2

The murder of the up-to-now unknown burgomaster of Aachen was in itself not a matter of great importance, especially as the Western Allies expected the war to end in a matter of weeks, perhaps even days. However, just like Skorzeny's failed mission of the previous December during the Battle of the Bulge, it created a tremendous scare in the alliance, especially among the American Top Brass. They were confident that soon they would have to rule an occupied country numbering some fifty million odd people. But how could they do so if a German resistance, on the same lines as the French maquis or the Polish Home Army, was on the rampage, supplied from the 'National Redoubt' in the Bavarian-Austrian Alps, where the Germans could hold out for years?

The feeling of despair in US Headquarters in Paris and Luxembourg was heightened when, in the last days of March, Goebbels' propaganda machine went into action to reveal all the details of the Werewolf Organization. On 29 March, 1945, the German Press Agency in Berlin announced boldly that the 'Burgomaster of Aachen, the lawyer Franz Oppenhoff', had been executed by the order of the 'German People's Court of Justice' because of 'collaboration with the enemy'.

This bold announcement, which was based on Allied reports in the *New York Times* and the London *Times*, was taken up immediately by the Nazi Press. The editorial writer of the *Flensburger Nachrichten* stated on 31 March: 'As reported by the official English news agency, Reuter, and confirmed by Allied military authorities, the Allied appointed burgomaster of Aachen Franz Oppenhoff was killed a few days ago by German freedom-fighters. We would like to add this information to the news. Oppenhoff was condemned to death by the "Court for the Preservation of German Honour" immediately he entered the service of the hated enemy'. The Berlin *Völkischer Beobachter*, Hitler's own paper, took up the same theme, commenting: 'A dishonourable, treacherous creature deserved the fate he brought upon himself by his actions. And in the future anyone who infringes the higher law of the land, the law of national honour and loyalty, will inevitably meet the same fate.'

In that last week of March the German Press was full of tales, real and imaginary, calculated to frighten Allied Intelligence into believing that the Allies would be forced into fighting a pro-tracted partisan war once the real shooting war was over; and at the same time bolstering up the German will to resist to the 'last man and the last bullet'.

On 1 April the shock caused by the Oppenhoff murder in the Allied camp was heightened even more by the first broadcast of a new German radio station – *Radio Werwolf*. The new station had nothing to do with the organization led by Pruetzmann. It was the brainchild of Dr Goebbels. But Allied Intelligence didn't know that. They thought it was yet another part of the German resistance movement, akin to those inflammatory messages broadcast to the European resistance movements from London for years after 1940.

And *Radio Werwolf* was definitely inflammatory. Time and again it hammered out the twin message of hate, '*Destroy the enemy or destroy yourself!* Civilian or soldier, whether you are still unoccupied or deep behind enemy lines, fight on!'

'There is no end to revolution,' *Radio Werwolf* declared, 'A revolution is only doomed to failure if those who make it cease to be revolutionaries. Together with the monuments to culture, there crumble the last obstacles to the fulfilment of our revol-utionary task. Now that everything is in ruins we are forced to rebuild Europe. In the past private possessions led us to restraint. Now the bombs, instead of killing all Europeans, have only smashed the prison walls which kept them captive. In trying to destroy Europe the enemy has only succeeded in smashing the past; and with that everything old and outworn has gone.'

It was the true nihilistic voice of the Nazi creed, the only

159

authentic voice of Nazism, whose leaders generally had grown fat and content in their good years of absolute power. But although it was only Geobbels speaking and not the mass of the German people, such broadcasts began to frighten not only the Intelligence men but also America's military leaders in Europe. Their fears were supported by the imaginings of the US press back home. *Collier's*, a now defunct magazine, for instance, conjured up a gigantic guerrilla warfare camp being built near Bad Aussee, close to the Führer's home at Berchtesgaden. Here the future partisans were being trained. They would continue the war for years after any official German surrender. Press comment of this type grew in volume and was supported by such trusted correspondents and commentators as Drew Pearson and Victor Schuff, who maintained that 'Hitler's henchmen in the east of Switzerland are expected to make a final stand.'

SHAEF Intelligence started to log all the details of this new 'Reported National Redoubt' on the wall of the map room at Eisenhower's HQ at Rheims. The map, which covered twenty thousand square miles of territory in Bavaria, Austria and Northern Italy, was soon filled with a rash of red marks indicating training schools, barracks, bunkers, etc, etc.

Eisenhower's Chief of Intelligence, General Strong, was basically a sceptic. But after an advancing US unit had captured a Werewolf document stating that the organization must 'recruit men of outstanding ability, experience and courage ... for its leaders', followed a little later by the capture of a Werewolf HQ, Strong was convinced that if something was not done soon, '[the Germans] would be in a position to set up a widespread network of Resistance posts which might well ... interfere with our operations.'

All that first week of April, 1945, Eisenhower wrestled with the problem of his future strategy. The Rhine had now been crossed in strength. What should be his final objective – Berlin or this new supposed threat, the National Redoubt?

In the end he selected the latter. As he wrote in his memoirs: 'Another Nazi purpose, somewhat akin to that of establishing a mountain fortress, was the organization of an underground arm, to which he gave the significant name of "Werewolves". The purpose of the Werewolf organization ... was murder and terrorism. Boys and girls as well as adults were to be absorbed into the secret organization with the hope of terrifying the countryside and making so difficult the problem of occupation that the conquering force would presumably be glad to get out.

'The way to stop this project – and such a development was always a possibility because of the passionate devotion to their Führer of many young Germans – was to overrun the entire national territory before its organization could be affected.'

So it was that, in the last weeks of the war, the Werewolf Organization with its mere four to five thousand members, mostly teenagers, determined, in part, Allied future war strategy and, as a result, helped to change the face of Europe for nearly half a century.

In essence, the assassination of Franz Oppenhoff and the Goebbels propaganda campaign which followed were a great coup. The Americans went off on a wild goose chase into Bavaria, while the glittering prize of Berlin was left to the Russians. The Werewolf movement, which had frightened Eisenhower so much that he changed his strategy, died a sudden death immediately Germany surrendered on 8 May, 1945. Germany, despite being committed to 'total war', was the only conquered country in Europe which didn't produce a resistance movement after defeat. Within two weeks of Germany's surrender, the Allied order for all troops in Germany to carry their personal weapon with them, on and off duty, was rescinded. There was no need. The average Tommy or GI was as safe in Germany's villages and towns as they were in their own country.

'As if,' General Siegfried Westphal, the last *Wehrmacht* chief of staff, said contemptuously after his capture that May, 'what the *Wehrmacht* had failed to do could be accomplished by a rabble of boy scouts.'

It was as fitting an epitaph on Hitler's Werewolves as any—'a rabble of boy scouts'.

Eleven: Death Comes to Father Christmas
1945

'*My dear fellow, I'm not reproaching you. Of course they were traitors. Canaris had even been passing on information to the Allies. They were all traitors, those Army swine, from the generals down.*'

Werewolf in The Odessa File *by F. Forsyth*

Back in 1918, when Canaris was languishing in an Italian jail as a suspected spy, one of his guards had come in grinning all over to inform the future admiral that he would hang '*dopodomani*', the day after tomorrow.

But that day didn't come. He was freed and would live for nearly another thirty years before that prophecy came true. Three times in all Canaris had been in prison and had walked out a free man. Now he was incarcerated for the fourth time. Would he go free again?

Schellenberg had arrested Canaris personally in the previous August. Old 'Father Christmas' had begged the younger spymaster to do his best for him. He said, 'You must promise me faithfully that within the next few days you will get me an opportunity to talk to Himmler personally. All the others – Kaltenbrunner and Mueller – are nothing but filthy butchers, out for my blood.'

Schellenberg promised he would, but he never did.

Now Canaris was confined in Flossenburg Concentration Camp, not far from the old border with Czechoslovakia. Kaltenbrunner, who hated Canaris, had ordered him there. Heydrich's successor had interrogated Canaris personally and found him to be 'a masochist, a sadist and a homosexual of both active and passive character at the same time.' Flossenburg, in Kaltenbrunner's opinion, would be the ideal place to have Canaris liquidated.

Here, in the camp built for 16,000 prisoners, but now housing 60,000, Canaris was held in the special 'bunker' reserved for high ranking German and foreign inmates. As were the others, Canaris was routinely beaten up and flogged. Once he was ordered to

165

strip naked and be prepared to be hanged. But there had, apparently, been some administrative mistake and he was allowed to go back to his cell, watched as always by an old opponent from Cell 21, Colonel Lunding of Danish Military Intelligence.

On the night of 8/9 April two SS thugs beat Canaris up and broke his nose. About two o'clock on the morning of the 9th he was dragged back to his cell. The sound of their boots and the rattle of Canaris' chain roused Lunding from a fitful doze. Lunding waited till the footsteps died away and then, in his stocking feet, he slid over to the wall of his cell which joined with Canaris'. He tapped on it with his tin mug. Canaris acknowledged and began tapping out a message, happy that somewhere in this living hell there was someone, whom he'd never see, but with whom he could share his last moments: 'It was my last interrogation I think. They beat me up again. I think they've broken my nose. Now I shall die for my Fatherland. I have a clear conscience. You understand that as an officer I did my duty when I tried to oppose the criminal stupidity with which Hitler led Germany to ruin.'

Lunding tapped back a few words of hope, though he knew Canaris hadn't a chance. One of the guards who had brought him back after the beating had made a quick spiral gesture to the other thug. That meant their victim would soon be 'going up the chimney', as the guards called the death ovens.

Canaris began tapping on the wall again. Lunding pressed his ear to the rough surface of the wall. This time the sound was fainter. His last sentence came through, his last known contact with the outer world, in which he had once played such a great role: 'It was all in vain. I knew Germany was finished in 1942.'

Lunding was awakened by the cry of a child. It was probably the baby daughter of the former Austrian Chancellor, Kurt von Schuschnigg, who was also imprisoned in the Bunker. (He survived to become an American college professor after the war.) At six harsh commands echoed down the corridor. Lunding got up and put his eye to the crack in the cell door. Through it he could see down the corridor to a window which overlooked the courtyard where the more important prisoners were strangled. In the last six months he had seen 900 unfortunates murdered there. Now he listened and watched as the SS thugs called 'der Nächste, *der Nächste'* (the next one) and the doomed men came obediently out of their cells.

So the little Admiral's life came to an end. The man who had started the Second World War with his Brandenburgers had died at the command of the man for whom he had made that war.

BIBLIOGRAPHY

W. Brockdorff: *Geheimkommandos des Ilten Weltkriegs*. Wels, Munich, 1967.

N. Ritter: *Deckname Dr Rantzau*. Hoffmann and Campe, Hamburg, 1972.

H. Hoehne: *Canaris*. Bertelsmann, Gutersloh, 1976.

L. Farago: *Game of Foxes*. Hodder, London, 1971.

C. Whiting: *Skorzeny*. Ballantine, New York, 1972.

C. Whiting: *SS Werewolf*. Leo Cooper, London, 1972.

K. Bartz: *The Downfall of the German Secret Service*. Kimber, London, 1956.

H. Spaeter: *Die Brandenburger*. Angerer. Munich, 1978.

O. Skorzeny: *Lebe Gefahrlich*. Ring Verlag, Munich, 1962.

E. Gehlen: *The Gehlen Memoirs*. Collins, London, 1972.

W. Hoettl: *The Secret Front*. Praeger, New York, 1960.

L. Mosley: *Foxhole in Cairo*. Panther, London, 1960.

J. Eppler: *Operation Condor*. Future, London, 1978.

C. Whiting: *Ardennes: The Secret War*. Century, London, 1984.

H. Malloy-Mason: *To Kill Hitler*. Sphere, London, 1978.

INDEX